Crash Course in Library Services to People with Disabilities

Recent Titles in
Libraries Unlimited Crash Course Series

Crash Course in Library Services to People with Disabilities

Ann Roberts and Richard J. Smith

Crash Course Series

AN IMPRINT OF ABC-CLIO, LLC
Santa Barbara, California • Denver, Colorado • Oxford, England

Library of Congress Cataloging-in-Publication Data
Roberts, Elizabeth Ann.
    Crash course in library services to people with disabilities /
Ann Roberts and Richard Smith.
        p. cm. — (Crash course series)
    Includes bibliographical references and index.
    ISBN 978-1-59158-767-5 (alk. paper)
    1. Libraries and people with disabilities—United States.
I. Smith, Richard J. (Richard James), 1951–   II. Title.
    Z711.92.H3R63   2010
    027.6'630973—dc22   2009023985

14   13   12   11   10   1   2   3   4   5

This book is also available on the World Wide Web as an eBook.
Visit www.abc-clio.com for details.

Libraries Unlimited
An Imprint of ABC-CLIO, LLC

ABC-CLIO, LLC
130 Cremona Drive, P.O. Box 1911
Santa Barbara, California 93116-1911

This book is printed on acid-free paper ∞
Manufactured in the United States of America

CONTENTS

A NOTE FROM THE EDITOR

The potential patrons described in this book are, in many ways, like any other patron. They need information and they come to the library in person or online to get that information. They anticipate being treated as you would treat any other patron. However, they are very different in many ways, and it is those differences we are trying to provide to you.

The very nature of these differences makes it imperative that we be sensitive to whether they can be misunderstood or considered politically incorrect. For this reason, we have gathered together information you need to read from the original sources and in the exact words you will find there. This is a reference for you to turn to when you have a question about meeting the needs of someone who is mentally or physically handicapped, is homeless, or is an aging adult. These are all patrons good librarians strive to serve. We hope we've given you the basics for serving them.

—Blanche Woolls

INTRODUCTION

SERVICE TO ALL

The new reference librarian noticed a particular, and particularly faithful, patron not long after she went to work in a medium-sized county library. A slightly stooped, slightly graying gentleman ambled toward the circulation desk one day with an awkward gait and a big grin on his face. "Oh lord, here comes Gerard," a staff person said under her breath, as she turned away to shuffle books on a cart.

"I want book about trains," the gentleman said in a loud voice, his words garbled and hard to understand. The teenagers at the computers stopped what they were doing and gawkcd.

"I'm sorry, sir. You want what?" asked the new librarian.

"I want book about trains." The voice was louder this time, and the grin had become a grimace. Everyone in the library stopped in one of those moments reserved for television commercials, when time stands still.

"You know, book about trains! Big book!" This time the garbled words came out in a shout, and the new librarian quickly did an OPAC (online public access catalog) search for "trains."

"Okay, let's go see if we can find the book that you want. Follow me," she said, leading the shuffling middle-aged man off into the stacks.

After looking through *several* books about trains, she and the patron finally arrived at *the* book, the one he was looking for, the one he would return to check out time and time again. It seemed that Gerard was a great lover of books, and of some books in particular—the book about trains was a favorite, as was one about 1950s diners, and airplanes. Gerard was fond of oversized picture books and checked out the same books over and over, sometimes returning one set only to check out the stack that he had just returned two weeks before. He was a faithful patron who loved books, and who knew his own tastes, and the librarian could respect that. She liked books, too, and certainly wouldn't read just any old thing.

It didn't take long for the other staff members to decide that maybe Gerard wasn't such a pain after all—he knew what he liked, he always had his library card, and he and his caretaker returned his books on time. It wasn't long before everyone started greeting him with a big, "Hey, Gerard" every time he came through the door. He was a part of the local community and he deserved no less than an enthusiastic greeting when he walked through the library doors.

PEOPLE FIRST

A most important thing to remember when working with or talking about people with disabilities is that they are people first. The disability does not define the person, a person is not his or her disability, and that is an important distinction. In the often quoted and frequently paraphrased words of Mark Twain, the great American author and philosopher, "The difference between the almost right word and the right word 'tis really a large matter—it's the difference between the lightning bug and the lightning" (Twain, 1888). Using the right words to describe a person with disabilities does make a difference. Kathie Snow knows all about what it means to have a loved one defined by perceived differences. She is the creator of People First Language, which we share here. Her Disability is Natural Web site was created to encourage new ways of thinking about disability and to help create a society in which all people are valued and included.

Here is a little of Kathie's story: Kathie is the wife of Mark, the mother of Emily and Benjamin, and a zealous promoter of new ways of thinking about disability. Her first book, *Disability Is Natural: Revolutionary Common Sense for Raising Successful Children with Disabilities*, was published in 2001; the second edition was published in 2005. Her second book, *101 Reproducible Articles for a New Disability Paradigm,* was published in 2007.

Kathie's interest in disability issues began in 1987, when Benjamin was diagnosed with cerebral palsy at the age of four months. Today, Benjamin attends community college, was recently inducted into Phi Theta Kappa (the national honor society of community colleges), has won a national film award, and lives the life of his dreams. During the 2004 presidential election, Benjamin became interested in the political process, and his interest grew with the 2008 election. He registered as a Democrat, and became active in Senator Obama's campaign. He was first named a precinct captain of the Obama campaign, became the Democratic co-chair of his voting precinct, and was then elected to be an Obama delegate to the Colorado State Democratic Convention. Benjamin's achievements, however, were not part of the package at the time of his disability diagnosis. On her Web site, DisabilityIsNatural. com, Kathie writes:

> I was like most parents in similar situations—initially bewildered and somewhat frightened. And as many other parents do, I eagerly entered the world of services, interventions, and expert opinions—what I now call Disability World. . . . At first, I felt the relief that comes from the protective arms of early intervention (therapists, service coordinators, etc.). . . . Within a year, however, I began to question the conventional wisdom of Disability World. . . . In 1990, when Benjamin was three, I was a participant in Texas Partners in Policymaking, a leadership program for adults with developmental disabilities and parents of children with developmental disabilities. The Partners program (www.partnersinpolicymaking.com) featured state-of-the-art training presented by a variety of different instructors. But just as important were the valuable

lessons I learned from my classmates, especially the adults with developmental disabilities. The Partners training was life-changing, and it validated my hopes and beliefs that my son and others with disabilities, and their families, could enjoy rich, full, *ordinary* lives. (Snow, n.d.)

With wisdom gleaned from the trainers, her classmates, and her own son, Kathie and her family left Disability World behind and took their rightful places in the Real World.

Upon her graduation from Partners in 1991, Kathie wrote an article about the importance of using People First Language, she and her family moved to Colorado, and she was invited to speak to the next class of trainees in the Texas Partners program. The rest, as they say, is history. Invitations from Partners programs in 25 other states followed, and her career as a trainer and public speaker on disability issues blossomed. Kathie has updated her People First Language article on a regular basis, and it has been included on a variety of other Web sites, in newsletters, and training materials.

In her People First Language article, Kathie asks the question: Who are the so-called handicapped or "disabled? "Contrary to conventional wisdom, individuals with disabilities are not:

People who suffer from the tragedy of birth defects.
Paraplegic heroes who struggle to become normal again.
Victims who fight to overcome their challenges.
Nor are they the retarded, autistic, blind, deaf, learning disabled, etc.—ad nauseam!

They are people: moms and dads; sons and daughters; employees and employers; friends and neighbors; students and teachers; scientists, reporters, doctors, actors, presidents, and more. People with disabilities are people, *first.*" (Snow, 2009)

When referring to those who are different in some way, with some perceived disability, Kathie suggests, in keeping with People First Language, that we should always:

Say:	Instead of:
People with disabilities.	The handicapped or disabled.
Paul has a cognitive disability (diagnosis).	He's mentally retarded.
Kate has autism (or a diagnosis of . . .).	She's autistic.
Ryan has Down syndrome (or a diagnosis of . . .).	He's Down's; a Down's person; a mongoloid.
Sara has a learning disability (diagnosis).	She's learning disabled.
Bob has a physical disability (diagnosis).	He's a quadriplegic/is crippled.

Mary is of short stature/Mary's a little person.	She's a dwarf/midget.
Tom has a mental health condition.	He's emotionally disturbed/ mentally ill.
Nora uses a wheelchair/mobility chair.	She's confined to/is wheelchair bound.
Steve receives special ed services.	He's in special ed; is a sped student/inclusion student.
Tonya has a developmental delay.	She's developmentally delayed.
Children without disabilities.	Normal/healthy/typical kids.
Communicates with her eyes/device/etc.	Is non-verbal.
Customer	Client, consumer, recipient, etc.
Congenital disability.	Birth defect.
Brain injury.	Brain damaged.
Accessible parking, hotel room, etc.	Handicapped parking, hotel room, etc.
She needs . . . or she uses	She has problems with . . . / She has special needs. (Snow, 2009)

Describing the person first puts the emphasis on what is important about an individual, and using the right terminology is indeed the difference between the lightning and the lightning bug.

Over the next few pages, we hope to make you more aware of the ways in which you and your library can focus on providing effective library services to those with different needs and to help you feel confident and happy in doing so.

CHAPTER 1

Taking Stock

In the November 2008 newsletter of *Disability Is Natural,* Kathie Snow challenges her readers to question themselves regarding their attitudes toward persons with disabilities.

As librarians we are accustomed to the questions of others and questioning on our own part. We are constantly seeking for answers to questions big and small. If we question our attitudes about how we serve those with disabilities, we might find that there is yet much work to be done.

Don't be fooled into thinking only a small number of the U.S. population has disabilities. According to the Alliance for Technology Access (ATA), "At nearly twenty percent, people with disabilities are this country's largest minority. Couple this with an aging population who will increasingly experience vision, hearing, and mobility limitations and it is clear that this is a critical time in the evolution of our society and the ways that we respond to the diverse needs of this growing population" (ATA, 2002). The numbers of persons with disabilities will increase as the Baby Boomers age.

Making library services and programs accessible and visible is not something that happens quickly, by accident, or by magic. Librarians should view accessibility and inclusion as part of their mission and include statements regarding these issues in their policies and mission statements. Providing access is part of the library service continuum, and, as such, access to services requires vigilance, dedication, and funding.

Question Yourself!

Revolutionary Common Sense by Kathie Snow, www.disabilityisnatural.com

Perhaps we're in another age of enlightenment, and that would be a great thing. In the last few years, I've seen or heard the following expressions as book titles, on bumper stickers, and in other places:

—What If Everything You Knew Was Wrong—
—Don't Believe Everything You Think—
—Thinking Errors—

And I've recently read two fascinating books: *Sway: The Irresistible Pull of Irrational Behavior* by Ori Brafman and Rom Brafman, and *Mistakes Were Made (But Not By Me): Why We Justify Foolish Beliefs, Bad Decisions, and Hurtful Acts* by Carol Tavris and Elliot Aronson. Like the phrases above, these books ask the reader to question assumptions and beliefs. Wendell Johnson's decades-older book, *People in Quandaries: The Semantics of Personal Adjustment,* also encourages us to rethink our beliefs and the language we use. None of these books is specific to disability issues, but each has valuable lessons we can apply.

In the *Sway* book, the authors describe the "diagnosis bias" this way: "… the moment we label a person or a situation, we put on blinders to all evidence that contradicts our diagnosis." They also describe "value attribution," in which we "imbue someone … with certain qualities based on perceived value, rather than on objective data." And they include this quote from psychologist Franz Epting about what happens when people are labeled: "It's easy to start acting it out as a way of being in the world … And then it becomes quite a tangle between what's really going on with us versus what we have been labeled with."

In the *Mistakes Were Made* book, the authors share this profound wisdom: "… if we have enslaved members of another group, deprived them of decent education or jobs, kept them from encroaching on our professional turfs, or denied them their human rights, then we evoke stereotypes about them to justify our actions. By convincing ourselves that they are unworthy,

unteachable, incompetent, inherently math-challenged, immoral, sinful, stupid, or even subhuman, we avoid feeling guilty or unethical about how we treat them. And we certainly avoid feeling that we are prejudiced." They also describe the "confirmation bias" this way: "Once a detective decides that he or she has found the killer, the confirmation bias sees to it that the prime suspect becomes the only suspect."

Finally, in the *People in Quandaries* book, author Wendell Johnson states, "To talk of a person as belonging to this or that type, or possessing this or that quality, seldom does justice to the complexity and ever-changing character of the facts about him." Expanding on the labeling issue, Johnson writes, "When our classification, or labeling, of an individual determines, entirely and without exception, our attitudes and reaction toward that individual, our behavior is scarcely distinguishable from the behavior of Pavlov's dogs." And consider this gem from Johnson, who was a renowned professor at the University of Iowa, a speech pathologist, a psychologist, and a person who had a stutter: "There are some individuals who practically never ask a question. It seems not to occur to them that their information may be incomplete … Alfred Binet, the creator of the modern intelligence test, stressed the significance of self-criticism in his attempts to define intelligence."

So … *what if* everything we thought we knew about people with disabilities was wrong? What if we stopped *believing* everything we *think?* And what if we acknowledged, and then corrected, our *errors in thinking?* What are the implications of these issues for those of us who care about people with disabilities? What are the implications for people with disabilities? All of this is a lot to chew on …

How *does* a person's label or diagnosis affect our attitudes about and our actions toward the person? Do we put "blinders" on and see only the perceived limitations that accompany the diagnosis, ignoring positive and/or hopeful attributes or possibilities? Are our reactions automatic, like "Pavlov's dogs"?

How does "value attribution"—rather than "objective data"—impact our attitudes and actions? How, for example, does a diagnosis like "mental retardation" impact how we treat a person who has been given that diagnosis? Do we use assessments or evaluations to prove what we already believe to be true, or do we use them to discover new information? Have we ever questioned the results of assessment? What if they're wrong? Do we ever question a person's label or what that label means? And do we value/devalue this person over that person, based primarily on their diagnostic labels? Are those labeled "severe/profound" of less value than those labeled "mild/moderate"?

> Our Language Does our Thinking for Us.
> *Wendell Johnson*

How many of us "evoke stereotypes" about people to "justify our actions"? How many, for example, think they "know" that students in the "EBD [emotional-behavioral disorder] classroom" could "never" be in general ed classrooms? The EBD stereotype we embrace justifies our decision to segregate those students. Or, how many people operate from the "fact" that someone with an IQ below 70 could "never" live on his own? When we engage in actions that are harmful to others—like segregating people with disabilities, punishing them in the name of "treatment," and more—and then justify these actions through the use of stereotypes, *what does this do to the core of our souls? (And what about the souls of people with disabilities?)* What might happen if we no longer embraced any stereotypes?

How many of us adhere to the "confirmation bias"? If we "know" a person's diagnosis, does everything we "see" about the person "confirm" the diagnosis? What if we looked with new eyes, and recognized, for example, that a child is doing this-or-that *because he's four,* and not because he has autism; or that an adult's "inappropriate behavior" is situational—*he doesn't like what's happening to him right now*—and the behavior is not a consequence of his diagnosis. What if we welcomed the "complexity and ever-changing character" of each unique individual?

What about people with disabilities? What effect does labeling have on the person who is labeled? Could a person's difficulties actually be the result of the person trying to fit in the "mold created by the diagnosis," and not the actual diagnosis? Many people with disabilities are "placed" —*immersed*—with others who share the same or similar diagnosis, in special ed classrooms, residential facilities, and other settings. When "immersed" this way, we shouldn't be surprised at how many people then learn "how to have more" autism, cognitive disabilities, behavioral diagnoses, etc.

How many opportunities are lost to a person with a disability because of the "blinders" we wear when we fall under the "irrational force" of the "diagnosis bias"? How does our valuation of (and subsequent treatment of) a person with a disability affect *his perception of his own value and worth as a human being?* How many parents allow their dreams for their children to evaporate because of the "diagnosis bias" and the value they associate with the diagnosis?

These are some of the questions we can ask ourselves—I hope you'll think of more. As the parent of a young man with a disability, I learned very early to question the experts' negative predictions about my son's future. Questioning *their* beliefs, however, helped me realize the value in questioning *my own* beliefs. This, in turn, led me to an on-going study of thinking, philosophy, language, and more. And that leads to a final musing about the excerpts above: do we ask enough questions, is our "information incomplete," and are we willing to try "self-criticism"? I'll never be 100 percent there; it's a life-long, self-reflective journey that requires time spent on being still … thinking … and questioning … But these are not what most of us seem to value. We cherish ACTION! Perhaps, however, our *actions* could be more virtuous and principled, we could have a more positive impact on the lives of peoples with disabilities, and our souls could reach a higher level of consciousness, if we spent more time being still … thinking … and questioning ourselves …

From *Crash Course in Library Services to People with Disabilities* by Ann Roberts and Richard Smith. Santa Barbara, CA: Libraries Unlimited. Copyright © 2010.

There are many issues to consider when planning for access to library services for those with disabilities, and the following steps should be considered essential in the planning process:

- Find out what persons with disabilities feel they need in terms of library services.
- Have a specific staff person or persons whose duties include library accessibility as part of their written job description. Remember the buck has to stop somewhere.
- Provide continuing education opportunities for your staff in this area.
- Develop a written access plan.
- Review and update this plan annually, just like you do for all your policies and plans.
- Most importantly, conduct outreach to persons with disabilities.

"Access to community programs and services is a civil rights and social justice issue for persons with disabilities. By establishing policies and practices that demonstrate your recognition of the rights of all people and your commitment to inclusion, you can have a dramatic effect on the lives of people with disabilities in your community!" (ATA, 2002).

We should start with what our own professional organization, the American Library Association (ALA), has to say about library services to persons with disabilities:

On January 16, 2001, ALA Council, the governing body of the American Library Association, unanimously approved the following policy. The policy was written by the Americans with Disabilities Act Assembly, a representational group administered by the Association of Specialized and Cooperative Library Agencies (ASCLA), a division of the American Library Association.

AMERICAN LIBRARY ASSOCIATION: LIBRARY SERVICES FOR PEOPLE WITH DISABILITIES POLICY

The American Library Association recognizes that people with disabilities are a large and neglected minority in the community and are severely underrepresented in the library profession. Disabilities cause many personal challenges. In addition, many persons with disabilities face economic inequity, illiteracy, cultural isolation, and discrimination in education, employment and the broad range of societal activities.

Libraries play a catalytic role in the lives of people with disabilities by facilitating their full participation in society. Libraries should use strategies based upon the principles of universal design to ensure that library policy, resources and services meet the needs of all people.

ALA, through its divisions, offices and units and through collaborations with outside associations and agencies is dedicated to eradicating inequities and improving attitudes toward and services and opportunities for people with disabilities.

For the purposes of this policy, "must" means "mandated by law and/or within ALA's control" and "should" means "it is strongly recommended that libraries make every effort to . . ."

1. The Scope of Disability Law

Providing equitable access for persons with disabilities to library facilities and services is required by Section 504 of the Rehabilitation Act of 1973, applicable state and local statutes and the Americans with Disabilities Act of 1990 (ADA). The ADA is the Civil Rights law affecting more Americans than any other. It was created to eliminate discrimination in many areas, including access to private and public services, employment, transportation and communication. Most libraries are covered by the ADA's Title I (Employment), Title II (Government Programs and Services) and Title III (Public Accommodations). Most libraries are also obligated under Section 504 and some have responsibilities under Section 508 and other laws as well.

2. Library Services

Libraries must not discriminate against individuals with disabilities and shall ensure that individuals with disabilities have equal access to library resources. To ensure such access, libraries may provide individuals with disabilities with services such as extended loan periods, waived late fines, extended reserve periods, library cards for proxies, books by mail, reference services by fax or email, home delivery service, remote access to the OPAC, remote electronic access to library resources, volunteer readers in the library, volunteer technology assistants in the library, American Sign Language (ASL) interpreter or realtime captioning at library programs, and radio reading services.

Libraries should include persons with disabilities as participants in the planning, implementing, and evaluating of library services, programs, and facilities.

3. Facilities

The ADA requires that both architectural barriers in existing facilities and communication barriers that are structural in nature be removed as long as such removal is "readily achievable." This means easily accomplished and able to be carried out without much difficulty or expense.

The ADA regulations specify the following examples of reasonable structural modifications: accessible parking, clear paths of travel to and throughout the facility, entrances with adequate, clear openings or automatic doors, handrails, ramps and elevators, accessible tables and public service desks, and accessible public conveniences such as restrooms, drinking fountains, public telephones and TTYs. Other reasonable modifications may include visible alarms in rest rooms and general usage areas and signs that have Braille and easily visible character size, font, contrast and finish.

One way to accommodate barriers to communication, as listed in the ADA regulations, is to make print materials available in alternative formats such as large type, audio recording, Braille, and electronic formats. Other reasonable modifications to communications may include providing an interpreter or realtime captioning services for public programs and reference services through TTY or other alternative methods. The ADA requires that modifications to communications must be provided as long as they are "reasonable," do not "fundamentally alter" the nature of the goods or services offered by the library, or result in an "undue burden" on the library.

4. Collections

Library materials must be accessible to all patrons including people with disabilities. Materials must be available to individuals with disabilities in a variety of formats and with accommodations, as long as the modified formats and accommodations are "reasonable," do not "fundamentally alter" the library's services, and do not place an "undue burden" on the library. Examples of accommodations include assistive technology, auxiliary devices and physical assistance.

Within the framework of the library's mission and collection policies, public, school, and academic library collections should include materials with accurate and up-to-date information on the spectrum of disabilities, disability issues, and services for people with disabilities, their families, and other concerned persons. Depending on the community being served, libraries may include related medical, health, and mental health information and information on legal rights, accommodations, and employment opportunities.

5. Assistive Technology

Well-planned technological solutions and access points, based on the concepts of universal design, are essential for effective use of information and other library services by all people. Libraries should work with people with disabilities, agencies, organizations and vendors to integrate assistive technology into their facilities and services to meet the needs of people with a broad range of disabilities, including learning, mobility, sensory and developmental disabilities. Library staff should be aware of how available technologies address disabilities and know how to assist all users with library technology.

6. Employment

ALA must work with employers in the public and private sectors to recruit people with disabilities into the library profession, first into library schools and then into employment at all levels within the profession.

Libraries must provide reasonable accommodations for qualified individuals with disabilities unless the library can show that the accommodations would impose an "undue hardship" on its operations. Libraries must also ensure that their policies and procedures are consistent with the ADA and other laws.

7. Library Education, Training and Professional Development

All graduate programs in library and information studies should require students to learn about accessibility issues, assistive technology, the needs of people with disabilities both as users and employees, and laws applicable to the rights of people with disabilities as they impact library services.

Libraries should provide training opportunities for all library employees and volunteers in order to sensitize them to issues affecting people with disabilities and to teach effective techniques for providing services for users with disabilities and for working with colleagues with disabilities.

8. ALA Conferences

ALA conferences held at facilities that are "public accommodations" (e.g., hotels and convention centers) must be accessible to participants with disabilities.

The association and its staff, members, exhibitors, and hospitality industry agents must consider the needs of conference participants with disabilities in the selection, planning, and layout of all conference facilities, especially meeting rooms and exhibit areas. ALA Conference Services Office and division offices offering conferences must make every effort to provide accessible accommodations as requested by individuals with special needs or alternative accessible arrangements must be made.

Conference programs and meetings focusing on the needs of, services to, or of particular interest to people with disabilities should have priority for central meeting locations in the convention/conference center or official conference hotels.

9. ALA Publications and Communications

All ALA publications, including books, journals, and correspondence, must be available in alternative formats including electronic text. The ALA Web site must conform to the currently accepted guidelines for accessibility, such as those issued by the World Wide Web Consortium. (ALA, 2001)

Used with Permission from the ALA.

The ALA set forth this policy to demonstrate its commitment as a professional organization to not only comply with ADA regulations but to encourage librarians everywhere to practice equitable access to library services and programs above and beyond what the law demands.

ASCLA, the Association of Specialized and Cooperative Library Associations (a division of ALA), has produced a toolkit, "Library Accessibility—What You Need to Know" (DeLatte, 2008). According to the ASCLA Web site, this "toolkit series of fifteen tipsheets was developed to help librarians in all types of libraries understand and manage access issues. These issues include but are not limited to: patrons who have cognitive, mental, or emotional illnesses; patrons with learning and/or developmental disabilities; patrons with service animals; patrons needing assistive technologies; and patrons with physical disabilities. Each tipsheet addresses a specific concern." You can find the accessibility toolkit at: http://www.ala.org/ala/mgrps/divs/ascla/asclaprotools/accessibilitytipsheets/default.cfm.

POLICY STATEMENTS AND THE REQUEST FOR ACCOMMODATION

Many libraries offer policy statements in regard to their services to person with disabilities, and some libraries require a request for accommodation form to be filled out prior to a visit from a patron who might require a special accommodation. The request for accommodation is frequently preceded with the library's policy statement. Here are a couple of examples of policy statements that we located online.

Americans with Disabilities Act Compliance Policy

Statement of Policy

The Julia L. Butterfield Memorial Library complies with the Americans with Disabilities Act of 1990, Public Law 101-336 (ADA), which prohibits discrimination on the basis of disability. The ADA, as applied to cities, counties, and other local governmental entities, requires that no qualified individual with a disability shall, on the basis of a disability, be denied the benefits of local government services, programs, or activities.

Accordingly, Julia L. Butterfield Memorial Library WILL:

- Take appropriate steps to ensure that communications with applicants, participants, and members of the public with disabilities are as effective as communications with others.
- Make reasonable accommodations in policies, practices, or procedures when necessary to avoid discrimination on the basis of disability, unless a fundamental alteration in a local government program would result.
- Operate its programs so that, when viewed in their entirety, they are readily accessible to and usable by individuals with disabilities. (Julia L. Butterfield Memorial Library, n.d.)

Amesbury Public Library

Requests for Accommodations for Library Programs

The Amesbury Public Library is sensitive to the needs of all of its patrons. To facilitate access to routine library services and resources, the Library seeks to provide reasonable accommodation upon request to the Library staff for patrons with disabilities during regular service hours.

The Library also conducts many program events open to all patrons. The library building, built in 1902, has some program areas which may not be accessible to all persons.

Patrons wishing to attend a program event who are unable to access the proposed program location may make a request for reasonable accommodation. In order to allow the Library sufficient time to make alternate program arrangements, it would be preferable for requests for accommodation to be made no less than one week prior to any such program event.

To request accommodation with regard to Library programs generally or specific program events, patrons may contact . . . Assistant Library Director . . . at 149 Main Street, Amesbury, MA, 01913. As noted above, it would be preferable for requests for accommodation for program events to be made not less than one week in advance of the program. The Assistant Library Director will then take such action as may be necessary, including, for example: rescheduling of the program event; relocation of the program event to an accessible site within the Library, subject to availability; or relocation of the program event to a site available elsewhere in the City. The Assistant Library Director will take appropriate steps to notify registered participants and the local media of the change of location.

Approved by the Board of Trustees, October 2008 (Amesbury Public Library, 2008)

If you would like to create a request for accommodation form for your library, we suggest that you keep it simple and make it friendly. Providing service is not a hardship!

(Your Library Name Here)

Reasonable Accommodation Request Form

Date of request _____

Name _____

Address _____

_____

Phone _____

What service, program, or activity are you requesting accommodation for?

_____

_____

Date of anticipated need for accommodation: _____

Help us understand how we might make your experience at our library a good one. What type of accommodation or assistance are you requesting?

_____

_____

_____

For help in completing this form contact (Name, Title) at (phone number) or (e-mail address).

_____

Signature _____   Date _____

Please return this completed form to (Name, Title) by (Date) and remember the (Name of Your Library Here) is here to serve you!

WHERE TO BEGIN

Library services for persons with disabilities vary from state to state and region to region. The New Jersey State Library offers an overview of different types of services available to persons with different types of disabilities on their Web site at http://www. njstatelib.org/LDB/Disabilities/dsequa2.php. These examples include:

Adaptive Technology Workplace

A work place designed for people with disabilities which provides: a computer that converts printed text to synthetic speech; a speech synthesizers to read computer screen; a talking word processing program (BEX) that enables a blind person to edit the text and translate computer code into braille; and one-on-one training to use adaptive technology which is provided by library staff and by several volunteers who are blind.

Service Center for People with Disabilities

A Service Center which contains materials, adaptive technology, and assistive devices for persons with disabilities and provides direct service to them. The Center targets services for: 1) people who are blind and visually disabled, speech and hearing impaired, learning disabled; 2) their families; and 3) staff from the organizations that serve them.

Information and Referral Service

- develop a collection of resource materials and a referral file or database for national, state and local organizations providing services for persons with disabilities
- receive newsletters from advocacy groups, government and nonprofit agencies
- collect and distributes giveaway brochures from advocacy groups and agencies
- post announcements of meetings and workshops
- maintain a collection of catalogs of adaptive technology and assistive devices

Job Information Center

The Center provides people with disabilities with information on support services and on employment and educational opportunities. Materials include: employment job bulletins; catalogs from colleges with supportive programs for students with disabilities; and a vertical file with materials on education, employment and support agencies for disabled persons. This Center also has brochures, newsletters and books on careers, education, job hunting, disability employment issues, skills, small businesses, literacy and tests.

Collection of Toys and Books

This collection may be used by parents who are referred by the schools. It can contain:

- a collection of toys for children with disabilities, their parents and teachers
- recently published books written for parents of children with disabilities
- fiction about children with special needs

Collection of Materials (Including Alternative Formats)

Circulating collection of materials on such topics as:

- handicapping conditions which covers treatment as well as educational and social aspects
- biographies and autobiographies about persons with disabilities
- books about and for children with disabilities
- deaf history and culture
- selecting toys for deaf children presented in American Sign Language
- assistance for parents to meet the demands of having a child with disabilities
- interviews with successful persons with disabilities (New Jersey State Library, 1999)

The New Jersey State Library also suggests that "bibliographies, guides to the library, and brochures should also be available in alternate formats. Audiotapes of these library publications can be made on a standard tape recorder. Large print versions of computer-generated materials can be made by increasing the type size. The text may also be downloaded on a floppy disk for those patrons that prefer to have electronic versions" (New Jersey State Library, 1999).

Many libraries offer a "collection of assistive devices for people who are visually impaired which includes magnifiers and aids to make reading, writing, card playing, and telephoning easier, etc. . . . In conjunction with the devices, [your library can] maintain a collection of catalogs from companies that sell assistive devices and adaptive technology" (New Jersey State Library, 1999). We will examine assistive technology in greater detail in Chapter 3.

THE DO-IT CENTER

The University of Washington in Seattle is the home of the DO-IT (Disabilities, Opportunities, Internetworking, and Technology) Center, which "serves to increase the participation of individuals with disabilities in challenging academic programs and careers. It promotes the use of computer and networking technologies to increase independence, productivity, and participation in education and employment" (University of Washington, n.d.).

The international DO-IT Center serves to:

- Increase the success of people with disabilities in college and careers.
- Promote the application of universal design to physical spaces, information technology, instruction, and services.
- Distribute publications and videos to freely use and reproduce for presentations and exhibits.
- Provide resources for students with disabilities, K–12 educators, postsecondary faculty and administrators, librarians, employers, and parents and mentors. (University of Washington, n.d.)

The DO-IT Center is "the recipient of the National Information Infrastructure Award in Education, the Golden Apple Award, the President's Award of Excellence in Mentoring, Catalyst, and other awards" (University of Washington, n.d.). Its purpose it to help "people achieve success with the support of Washington State, the federal government, foundations, corporations, and people like you" (University of Washington, n.d.).

DO-IT is directed by Sheryl Burgstahler. In an article by Burgstahler (2002), "Universal Access: Making Library Resources Accessible to Persons with Disabilities," she describes what it means for libraries to adhere to the principles of universal design, or design for everyone.

> Universal design means that, rather than design your services and facility for the average user, you design them for people with a broad range of abilities and disabilities. Keep in mind that patrons may have learning disabilities and visual, speech, hearing, and mobility impairments.
>
> Although a library cannot be expected to have specialized equipment for every type of disability, staff should be aware of the options for making library resources accessible and should make available equipment that they can anticipate will be used or is available at relatively low cost. In addition, develop a procedure to ensure a quick response to requests for accommodations to meet the needs of patrons with disabilities. (Burgstahler, 2002)

Once you have considered some adaptive technology issues, further questions are posed concerning other issues such as legal and access issues.

ISSUES TO CONSIDER

"The following information and questions can help guide you in making all of your library's programs and resources universally accessible and inviting to people with disabilities" (Burgstahler, 2002). They include legal issues, access issues, building access and environment, and others. These are placed in the form of questions for you to answer.

Legal Issues

Do you understand the legal issues? In the article, Burgstahler discusses the legal issues surrounding accessibility:

> Section 504 of the Rehabilitation Act of 1973 and the Americans with Disabilities Act of 1990 prohibit discrimination against individuals with disabilities. According to these laws, no otherwise qualified individual with a disability shall, solely by reason of his/her disability, be excluded from the participation in, be denied the benefits of, or be subjected to discrimination under any program or activity of a public entity.
>
> In general, "person with a disability" means "any person who has a physical or mental impairment which substantially limits one or more major life activities including walking, seeing, hearing, speaking, breathing, learning, and working, has a record of such an impairment, or is regarded as having such an impairment." (Burgstahler, 2002)

Building Access and Environment

While we've already discussed questioning our attitudes toward persons with disabilities, Burgstahler further offers a series of general questions that relate to accessibility issues. These questions related to the library building and environment, staff, services, and electronic resources may help guide you in making your library universally accessible.

- Are parking areas, pathways, and entrances to the building wheelchair-accessible?
- Are doorway openings at least 32 inches wide and doorway thresholds no higher than one half inch?
- Are aisles kept wide and clear for wheelchair users? Have protruding objects been removed or minimized for the safety of users who are visually impaired?
- Are all levels of the library connected via an accessible route of travel, or are there procedures to assist patrons with mobility impairments in retrieving materials from inaccessible locations?
- Are ramps and/or elevators provided as alternatives to stairs? Do elevators have both auditory and visual signals for floors? Are elevator controls marked in large print and Braille or raised notation? Can people seated in wheelchairs easily reach all elevator controls?
- Are wheelchair-accessible restrooms with well marked signs available in or near the library?
- Are service desks and facilities such as book returns wheelchair accessible?
- Are there ample high-contrast, large print directional signs throughout the library? Are shelf and stack identifiers provided in large print and Braille formats? Are call numbers on book spines printed in large type? Is equipment marked with large print and Braille labels?

- Are telecommunication devices for the deaf (TDD/TTY) available?
- Are library study rooms available for patrons with disabilities who need to bring personal equipment or who need the assistance of a reader?
- Are hearing protectors, private study rooms, or study carrels available for users who are distracted by noise and movement around them?

Library Staff

- Are staff aware of disability issues?
- Are staff trained in the use of telecommunication devices for the deaf (TTD/TTY) and adaptive computer technology provided in the library? Are there regular refresher courses to help staff keep their skills up-to-date?
- Are staff trained in policies and procedures for providing accommodations to patrons with disabilities? Are staff aware of services provided for people with disabilities?
- Are staff knowledgeable of other organizations, such as federally-funded talking book and Braille libraries, that provide information services to patrons with disabilities?
- Do public services staff wear large print, name badges?
- If there are staff members with sign language skills, are they identified to other staff members so that, when available, they can assist patrons who are deaf?

Library Services

- Does the library have a designated staff member and/or committee who coordinates services for patrons with disabilities, monitors adaptive technology developments, and responds to requests for accommodation?
- Are people with disabilities included in the library's board of trustees and committees? Are people with disabilities included in the library's access planning process?
- Does the library have a written description of services for patrons with disabilities, including procedures and information on how to request special accommodations? These policies and procedures should be advertised in the library and library publications.
- Are reference and circulation services available by phone, TTY/TDD, and electronic mail?
- Are resource delivery services available for patrons confined to their homes, retirement facilities, or hospitals?
- Are large print and Braille versions of library handouts and guides available?
- Are applications for the nationwide network of Talking Book and Braille Libraries available for print disabled patrons?
- Are reader and research assistants available to patrons with vision impairments?

- Are sign language interpretation services available by request for library sponsored events?
- Are large magnifying glasses available for patrons with low vision?

Adaptive Technology for Computers

The library won't have special equipment on hand for every type of disability. But you can anticipate the most commonly requested adaptive technology and have that available. Start with a few items at first, and add new technology as patrons request it. Here is a list of adaptive technology for computers and computer workstations to get you started.

- At least one adjustable table for each type of workstation in the library can assist patrons with mobility impairments or who use wheelchairs.
- Large print key labels can assist patrons with low vision.
- Software to enlarge screen images can assist patrons with low vision and learning disabilities.
- Large monitors of at least 17 inches can assist patrons with low vision and learning disabilities.
- A speech output system can be used by patrons with low vision, blindness, and learning disabilities.
- Braille conversion software and a Braille printer can assist patrons who are blind.
- Trackballs can assist those who have difficulty controlling a mouse.
- Wrist rests and key guards can assist some patrons with mobility impairments.

Electronic Resources

Be sure that the library's World Wide Web pages and other electronic resources are designed to be accessible to people with disabilities. Consider these items in ensuring accessible electronic resources.

- Do electronic resources with images and sound provide text alternatives to these formats? Is the design consistent with clear navigation paths?
- Can the library's electronic resources, including online catalogs, indexes, and full-text databases and CD-ROMs, be accessed with a variety of adaptive computer technologies such as screen readers and speech synthesis?
- Do collection development policy statements specifically state that electronic products should be evaluated for accessibility as part of the purchasing process?
- Do library Web page style guidelines require that pages be designed in an accessible format?
- Are librarians prepared to assist patrons with electronic resources that they cannot access by providing research consultations or materials in other formats? (Burgstahler, 2002)

Helpful Communication Hints

In addition to issues of access for the library, Burgstahler offers excellent general communication tips and guidelines for working with persons with disabilities. "When you are working with someone who has a disability, keep in mind that you are dealing with a person first. Other than this, there are no strict rules when it comes to relating to people with disabilities. Here are some helpful hints.

General Guidelines

- Treat people with disabilities with the same respect and consideration that you give others.
- Ask a person with a disability if he/she needs help before helping.
- Talk directly to the person with a disability, not through the person's companion.
- Refer to a person's disability only if it is relevant to the conversation.
- Avoid negative descriptions of a person's disability. For example, 'a person who uses a wheelchair' is more appropriate than 'a person confined to a wheel-chair.' Remember, in actuality, a wheelchair is not confining—it's liberating.
- Refer to the person first and then the disability. 'A man who is blind' is better than 'a blind man' because it emphasizes the person first.

Visual Impairments

- Be descriptive with people with visual impairments. Say, 'The computer is about three feet to your left,' rather than, 'The computer is over there.'
- When guiding people with visual impairments, offer them your arm rather than grabbing or pushing them.
- Always ask permission before you interact with a person's guide or service dog.

Learning Disabilities

- If asked, read instructions to users with some specific learning disability.

Mobility Impairments

- Try sitting in order to make level eye contact with patrons in wheelchairs when you interact.

Speech Impairments

- Listen carefully and ask people with speech impairments to repeat what they have said if you don't understand.

Hearing Impairments

- Face people with hearing impairments and speak clearly when you talk to them" (Burgstahler, 2002).

OTHER ACCOMMODATIONS

Have you ever been in a work or public situation where the introduction of someone in a wheelchair or using a service dog caused complete pandemonium? Unfortunately, it happens. People who are unprepared or unused to seeing a person in a wheelchair or using a service dog can just become unhinged! You and your library staff should be prepared not only to welcome and assist persons with disabilities but also to allow the service animals that they might use into the library. The U.S. Department of Justice Civil Rights Division Disability Rights Section has published "Commonly Asked Questions about Service Animals in Places of Business" at http://www.ada.gov/qasrvc.htm. The answers to these questions will help you formulate your own policies about service animals.

1. Q: What are the laws that apply to my business?

    A: Under the Americans with Disabilities Act (ADA), privately owned businesses that serve the public, such as restaurants, hotels, retail stores, taxicabs, theaters, concert halls, and sports facilities, are prohibited from discriminating against individuals with disabilities. The ADA requires these businesses to allow people with disabilities to bring their service animals onto business premises in whatever areas customers are generally allowed.

2. Q: What is a service animal?

    A: The ADA defines a service animal as any guide dog, signal dog, or other animal individually trained to provide assistance to an individual with a disability. If they meet this definition, animals are considered service animals under the ADA regardless of whether they have been licensed or certified by a state or local government. Service animals perform some of the functions and tasks that the individual with a disability cannot perform for him or herself. Guide dogs are one type of service animal, used by some individuals who are blind. This is the type of service animal with which most people are familiar. But there are service animals that assist persons with other kinds of disabilities in their day-to-day activities. Some examples include:

    Alerting persons with hearing impairments to sounds.
    Pulling wheelchairs or carrying and picking up things for persons with mobility impairments.
    Assisting persons with mobility impairments with balance.

    A service animal is not a pet.

3. Q: How can I tell if an animal is really a service animal and not just a pet?

    A: Some, but not all, service animals wear special collars and harnesses. Some, but not all, are licensed or certified and have identification papers. If you are not certain that an animal is a service animal, you may ask the person who has the animal if it is a service animal required because of a disability. However, an individual who is going to a restaurant or theater is not likely to be carrying documentation of his or her medical condition or disability. Therefore, such documentation generally may not be required as a condition for providing service to an individual accompanied by a service animal. Although a number of states have programs to certify service animals, you may not insist on proof of state certification before permitting the service animal to accompany the person with a disability.

4. Q: What must I do when an individual with a service animal comes to my business?

   A: The service animal must be permitted to accompany the individual with a disability to all areas of the facility where customers are normally allowed to go. An individual with a service animal may not be segregated from other customers.

5. Q: I have always had a clearly posted "no pets" policy at my establishment. Do I still have to allow service animals in?

   A: Yes. A service animal is not a pet. The ADA requires you to modify your "no pets" policy to allow the use of a service animal by a person with a disability. This does not mean you must abandon your "no pets" policy altogether but simply that you must make an exception to your general rule for service animals.

6. Q: My county health department has told me that only a guide dog has to be admitted. If I follow those regulations, am I violating the ADA?

   A: Yes, if you refuse to admit any other type of service animal on the basis of local health department regulations or other state or local laws. The ADA provides greater protection for individuals with disabilities and so it takes priority over the local or state laws or regulations.

7. Q: Can I charge a maintenance or cleaning fee for customers who bring service animals into my business?

   A: No. Neither a deposit nor a surcharge may be imposed on an individual with a disability as a condition to allowing a service animal to accompany the individual with a disability, even if deposits are routinely required for pets. However, a public accommodation may charge its customers with disabilities if a service animal causes damage so long as it is the regular practice of the entity to charge non-disabled customers for the same types of damages. For example, a hotel can charge a guest with a disability for the cost of repairing or cleaning furniture damaged by a service animal if it is the hotel's policy to charge when non-disabled guests cause such damage.

8. Q: Am I responsible for the animal while the person with a disability is in my library?

   A: No. The care or supervision of a service animal is solely the responsibility of the owner. You are not required to provide care or food or a special location for the animal.

9. Q: What if a service animal barks or growls at other people, or otherwise acts out of control?

   A: You may exclude any animal, including a service animal, from your facility when that animal's behavior poses a direct threat to the health or safety of others. For example, any service animal that displays vicious behavior towards other guests or customers may be excluded. You may not make assumptions, however, about how a particular animal is likely to behave based on your past experience with other animals. Each situation must be considered individually. Although a public accommodation may exclude any service animal that is out of control, it should give the individual with a disability who uses the service animal the option of continuing to enjoy its goods and services without having the service animal on the premises.

10. Q: Can I exclude an animal that doesn't really seem dangerous but is disruptive to my business?

    A: There may be a few circumstances when a public accommodation is not required to accommodate a service animal—that is, when doing so would result in a fundamental alteration to the nature of the business. [Generally, this is not likely to occur, but when it does, for example, when a dog barks during a storytime, the animal can be excluded.] If you have further questions about service animals or other requirements of the ADA, you may call the U.S. Department of Justice's toll-free ADA Information Line at 800-514-0301 (voice) or 800-514-0383 (TDD). (U.S. Department of Justice, 1996)

GETTING IN ON THE GROUND FLOOR

In "Educating Students to Serve Information Seekers with Disabilities" (Walling, 2004), Linda Lucas Walling, suggests that schools of library and information science are not doing a very good job of equipping new library school graduates with the tools they need to serve persons with disabilities.

Walling asserts that with the passage of the ADA in 1990 and subsequent revisions to Section 508 of the Rehabilitation Act, library and information science (LIS) programs have a responsibility to make their students not only aware of the law but of their responsibility and charge to serve the persons with disabilities in their local community.

The article reports on a survey conducted in 2000, which looked at how LIS programs provide education related to ADA, services for persons with disabilities, and adaptive technologies. The survey was sent to the deans and directors of all ALA-accredited LIS programs and requested information about whether education is provided about these topics and, if it is provided, how and where is it provided.

While there has been significant progress made in this area, 10 years after the passage of the ADA, only 66 percent of the responding schools ensure that all of their graduates know about the law, and about a quarter of the responding schools offer instruction only in elective courses, with only two-thirds of the responding programs ensuring that all of their graduates are exposed to information about the ADA's provisions. Walling's study also revealed that only 58 percent of the responding programs ensure that all of their graduates are exposed to information about services for persons with disabilities, suggesting that only the bare bones provisions of the law are mentioned briefly in those programs that offer information about ADA but not about services.

An even smaller percentage of LIS programs, slightly more than half, reported that all of their students are exposed to information about adaptive technology, and some of the programs viewed adaptive technology as associated only with school library media centers or public and academic libraries, not the general public. As Walling states in the article, "This suggests a misunderstanding of the implications of the technology for all information agencies and all information seekers" (Walling, 2004, p. 145).

Walling suggests that in order to ensure that persons with disabilities are viewed as part of the overall population of library users, LIS programs must view services for this portion of the population as one of their own personal core values. LIS programs must be aware of the requirements of ADA and the barriers to information that people with various disabilities experience and ensure that their students come in contact with course content that includes examples of information needs and information seeking of persons with disabilities, including discussion of alternative methods for service delivery, alternative formats, and resources for identifying and accessing them. Walling recommends that a discussion of the programs and services of the National Library Service (NLS) for the Blind and Physically Handicapped should be mandatory in all LIS programs and that accessible Web design and assistive and adaptive technologies should have a place in every LIS curriculum.

Ensuring that librarians are able to explain the nuances of People First Language, developed by Kathie Snow, and promote its use among faculty and students will guarantee that graduates of LIS programs view library users with disabilities as a type of user, not as special populations to be served by someone else. Getting in on the ground floor with new graduates of library programs is the best way to ensure that libraries everywhere are doing their part to serve this portion of the population.

DISABLED OR DISLABELED?

According to "Those of Us Dislabeled: A Guide to Awareness and Understanding" (Sheppard-Jones, 2000), there are simple things that all of us can do to help eliminate barriers for persons with disabilities:

1. Encourage the participation of people with disabilities in community activities by making sure that meeting and event sites are accessible.
2. Understand children's curiosity about disabilities and people who have them.
3. Speak up when negative words or phrases are used in connection with disability.
4. Accept people with disabilities as individuals with the same needs and feelings you have. Your mother was right when she told you to treat people the way you want to be treated.
5. Understand the reason for accessible parking and leave it for those who need it.
6. Hire qualified persons with disabilities. (Sheppard-Jones, 2000)

CONCLUSION

Putting the person first in dealing with persons with disabilities is the bedrock for forming policies and setting standards in your library. If your library is very small with a very small budget, carrying out any remodeling suggested here will take some long-term planning. You may not be able to help through educating students of library and information technology about assistive technology and disability issues to help pave the way for excellence in service to this underserved population, but making yourself and your staff aware of the very basic issues and the requirements that you can implement will be a good start. It's called the golden rule, and this rule is one to live by, in our personal and professional lives.

CHAPTER 2

Leading by Example

While one can find many examples of services for persons with disabilities, as well as some examples of programming that targets this library user population, there are not nearly enough. Let's say that you're inspired to start a program or service of your own, and you need a compelling argument to convince board and staff to join in the effort, but you don't know where to start. It might be a good idea to determine the size of your local population of persons with disabilities. Get together a few statistics to add to the heartfelt rhetoric you'll be using to convince the reluctant ones.

THE NUMBERS

So how do we find statistics about the number of persons with disabilities and potential library users in our communities? In the article "Use of Statistics from National Data Sources to Inform Rehabilitation Program Planning, Evaluation, and Advocacy" (Bruyere & Houtenville, 2006), we find some suggestions for using different data sources for collecting data on persons with disabilities. Although this article specifically addresses the use of data for the purposes of rehabilitation services, you can use these data collection methods in the process of advocacy for and marketing to this portion of the population. In this article, the authors describe the array of available data and statistics and their potential uses in rehabilitation service planning and evaluation. They discuss the most widely accessible surveys, which might be the most useful for librarians, the 2000 Decennial Census Long Form and the American Community Survey (ACS). The ACS is a nationwide survey that collects socioeconomic and housing information and is the planned replacement for the long form in the 2010 Census. The U.S. Census Bureau plans to conduct the ACS in every county, American Indian and Alaska Native Area, Hawaiian Home Land, and in Puerto Rico, once it is fully implemented, pending Congressional funding. The ACS has been tested across the country since 1996.

The Decennial Census Long Form

The 2000 Census is the primary source of local-level statistics on people with disabilities measured consistently across the country. One in six households received the long form in 2000, which contains demographic and other relevant questions, such as information about living arrangements, employment, income, transportation utilization, and housing. The six questions appearing on the Census 2000 long form regarding disability are shown below so you will know the type of information you would have at your disposal:

- Does this person have any of the following long-lasting conditions:

    a. Blindness, deafness, or a severe vision or hearing impairment?
    b. A condition that substantially limits one or more basic physical activities such as walking, climbing stairs, reaching, lifting, or carrying?

    Yes _____   No _____

- Because of a physical, mental, or emotional condition lasting 6 months or more, does this person have any difficulty in doing any of the following activities:

    a. Learning, remembering, or concentrating?
    b. Dressing, bathing, or getting around inside the home?
    c. (Answer if this person is 16 YEARS OLD OR OVER.) Going outside the home alone to shop or visit a doctor's office?
    d. (Answer if this person is 16 YEARS OLD OR OVER.) Working at a job or business?

    Yes _____   No _____   (U.S. Census Bureau, 2000)

The 2000 Census "counted 49.7 million people with some type of long lasting condition or disability. They represented 19.3 percent of the 257.2 million people who were aged 5 and older in the civilian noninstitutionalized population—or nearly one person in five" (U.S. Census Bureau, 2003). The 2000 Census also revealed that there were:

- 9.3 million (3.6 percent) with a sensory disability involving sight or hearing.
- 21.2 million (8.2 percent) with a condition limiting basic physical activities, such as walking, climbing stairs, reaching, lifting, or carrying.
- 12.4 million (4.8 percent) with a physical, mental, or emotional condition causing difficulty in learning, remembering, or concentrating.
- 6.8 million (2.6 percent) persons with a physical, mental, or emotional condition causing difficulty in dressing, bathing, or getting around inside the home.
- 18.2 million of those aged 16 and older with a condition that made it difficult to go outside the home to shop or visit a doctor (8.6 percent of 212.0 million people this age).
- 21.3 million of those aged 16 to 64 with a condition that affected their ability to work at a job or business (11.9 percent of the 178.7 million people this age). (U.S. Census Bureau, 2003)

Many administrative uses are made of Census disability statistics, and according to the Census Bureau, these data are used widely by federal and community decision makers under several programs. Data is used "to distribute funds and develop programs for people with disabilities and the elderly under the Rehabilitation Act; to distribute funds for housing for people with disabilities under the Housing and Urban Development Act; to allocate funds to states and local areas for employment and job training programs for veterans under the Job Training Partnership Act, Disabled Veterans Outreach Programs" (National Council on Disability, 2001) among other things. If you are seeking information about the number of persons with disabilities in your community, you can obtain the same type of statistical information for your own purposes. If nothing else is available, The American FactFinder (at http://factfinder.census.gov) allows users to search by ZIP code. You can easily locate demographical information about the community surrounding your library.

KNOW YOUR RESOURCES

Persons with disabilities often need help with the simplest things, such as where to find housing that they can actually navigate or how to make sure that a certain test that they'd like to take is accessible to them. Federal, state, and local government agencies all provide various services for those with disabilities, and it is important for your library to provide information about those services. We are, after all, information providers. The federal government has a Web site, Disability.gov, which is searchable by state, and located at: http://www.disability.gov/

Disability.gov provides quick and easy access to comprehensive information about disability programs, services, laws, and benefits. You can begin your search by visiting any of the 10 subject areas listed in the left-hand menu on this page. To find disability resources in your state, just click the "Information by State" drop-down menu located in the left-hand menu, and highlighted in red. Some of the many topics you will find information about on Disability.gov include the following:

- Americans with Disabilities Act (ADA)
- Autism and other developmental disabilities
- Fair housing rights
- Social Security disability benefits
- Vocational rehabilitation

The Missouri Governor's Council on Disability provides a searchable database of resources for persons with disabilities within that state, and it is searchable by type of service required, organization, type of disability, and county. While no single agency can provide one-stop shopping for services to those with disabilities, some of the online directories come pretty close and would be the most often updated, as opposed to print directories. Municipal governments frequently have publications or online information regarding housing or other services. Have a list of local services available for those patrons with disabilities in various formats, update it often, and make sure that everyone on your staff knows where to find this resource.

MARKETING YOUR LIBRARY'S SERVICE TO PERSONS WITH DISABILITIES

The New Jersey State Library also offers excellent suggestions for marketing your services to persons with disabilities. At the very least, your library should "develop a brochure describing the library's services for persons with disabilities and mail it to agencies that serve this population" (New Jersey State Library, 1999). If time, staffing, and budget allow, you might "develop individual brochures for people who are deaf, blind, have low vision, have learning disabilities, etc. Include in the brochure a list of library materials, programs, services, adaptive technology and any electronic full-text information that is available on the library's web site. . . . Develop a display which highlights library services for people with disabilities" (New Jersey State Library, 1999) and place it in a prime location where everyone who visits your library will become aware of those services.

Another way of marketing is to "visit parent groups, sign language classes, clubs, local government and community service agencies, etc." (New Jersey State Library, 1999) to forge relationships with the organizations that work with persons with disabilities. Another suggestion is that if you are really serious about reaching out to this portion of the population, you should also "participate in open houses and resource fairs organized by other agencies" (New Jersey State Library, 1999). Forging relationships with these agencies is not only an excellent way to market but also will help you build your library programs.

Yet another simple means of marketing, a practice that is already common in many libraries, is to develop bibliographies for distribution of the following:

- Books on disabilities
- Titles of magazines and newsletters focusing on disabilities
- Books on toys and play for children with special needs
- Employment opportunities for persons with disabilities
- Biographies and autobiographies about persons with disabilities (New Jersey State Library, 1999)

Always encourage readers with low vision or with physical handicaps that make reading difficult to sign up for the state or regional talking book services, which are affiliates of the National Library Service (NLS) for the Blind and Physically Handicapped in Washington, DC. We'll discuss the services offered by the NLS in Chapter 6.

PERFECT PARTNERS: A SPECIAL NEEDS LENDING LIBRARY

In Holmes County, Ohio, the Holmes County District Public Library and the Holmes County Training Center (HCTC), a program to assist people with developmental and mental disabilities, joined together to create a special needs lending library, with local funds and a library services and technology grant from the Ohio State Library. The new lending library was dedicated in 2007 and is open to any person with a disability or their caregiver living or working in Holmes County. According to an article in *The Holmes Bargain Hunter* (Mast, 2007), the HCTC had a parent resource prior to the grant award, but it was unorganized and outdated. The librarians saw this partnership as a good opportunity to reach out to a local underserved population: the developmentally disabled and their caregivers. "This joint effort between the Holmes County Board of MR/DD [Mental Retardation and Development Disabilities] and the Holmes County District Public Library to establish the Special Needs Lending Library meets our mission to provide services to the disabled and their caregivers and meets our goal of reaching out to all of the disabled in the community and provide them access to the resources provided through this project" (Holmes County District Public Library, 2007).

The lending library offers print collections including the following:

- Resources for professionals working with the disabled
- Parent/teacher resources on developmental disabilities
- Audio-visual training materials
- Children's picture books

- Adaptive toy collection geared toward developmental education of children and adults with disabilities
- Internet-enabled computer workstation (Holmes County District Public Library, 2007)

"The public access computer can be used to place holds on items available through the library's online catalog; to search the library's premium databases; and to search the internet for materials on living and working with those with disabilities" (Holmes County District Public Library, 2007).

Usage Guidelines at the HCTC Special Needs Lending Library

- All materials, including books and toys must be checked out using a valid Holmes County District Public Library card.
- All materials check out for 28 days and must be renewed once as long as no one is waiting for the item.
- Fines will not accrue on items checked out, but overdue notices and bills for lost or damaged items will be generated. Since the collections are limited, please return materials promptly.
- The primary purpose of the Special Needs Lending Library is to serve the disabled and their caregivers.
- The Adaptive Toy collection may only be borrowed by residents of Holmes County and can be reserved for pickup at any Holmes County District Public Library location or bookmobile stop.
- Within Holmes County, resource materials and toys can be requested form the online catalog and delivered to Holmes County District Public Library locations via our CARGO delivery system.
- To access the Special Needs Lending Library, please sign in at the main office at the Training Center.
- If no staff member is available in the Special Needs Lending Library, please go to the main office for assistance.
- The Special Needs Lending Library will be staffed part-time by an employee of the Holmes County Training Center.
- When a staff member is not present, please check out materials using the self-check computer.
- If you do not have a valid Holmes County District Public Library card, you may apply for one with the staff member on duty or visit any Holmes County District Public Library location to register. (Holmes County District Public Library, 2007)

According to the article by Mast, the Special Needs Lending Library in Holmes County, Ohio, was visited by Michele Farrell, senior program officer for the Institute of Museum and Library Services (IMLS), as part of a general tour of libraries that have received funding from the IMLS, who said of the project: "It is a fantastic library, and one which we are proud to be able to say that we were a part of supporting. It's libraries like these which are a joy to come out and see how they have made a very positive impact on their community and on their state" (Mast, 2007). Through local and federal funding, a public library and a local agency dedicated to serving persons with disabilities were able to create a unique partnership and a lending library that has boosted services to an underserved population.

IN-HOME LIBRARY SERVICES

In "Homebound Services: Old Ways and New Ways," Theresa Gemmer (2003) suggests that library service in the home should not be called "homebound" or "shut-in" service but "home library service." We prefer the term "in-home library service." Many people taking advantage of in-home library service are elderly persons and persons with disabilities living at home who are still able to leave the home, perhaps with assistance from a friend or relative or public transit system. While libraries do serve people who are unable to leave their homes, a large number of home library service patrons fall into the category of those who are able to leave the home but might find it difficult to do so.

As with any library service, it is necessary to define the user group that is eligible for in-home library service, to establish policies, and to market the service. The Hennepin County Library in suburban Minneapolis, Minnesota, not only offers in-home service to patrons but produces a bimonthly newsletter, called *At Home Reader,* which features book reviews, listings of new materials, and news items of interest about the library. Here is how Hennepin County Library promotes their library service at home through the library's Web site.

Hennepin County Library Makes House Calls!

The At Home Service is provided to residents who can not visit a library due to illness, disability, visual impairment.

Here's how it works:

Materials and services are delivered in person by a volunteer or sent through the U.S mail, at no charge to you with return postage paid. The At Home Service provides you with access to a wide range of materials and services from the Hennepin County Library, such as:

- Large print and regular print books, including current best sellers
- Audio books and compact discs, both abridged and unabridged version of books
- Video tapes and DVDs
- Music on CD
- Magazine and newspaper articles
- Information from the Internet
- Answers to informational questions located by the department's librarians (Hennepin County Library, n.d.b)

Hennepin County Library allows patrons to apply for in home service online, by phone, or through the mail, with an application that allows users to sign up for the service temporarily, as in the case of an illness or recovery from surgery, or for ongoing service for visual impairment, illness, or other disability.

Getting Started with In-Home Library Service

When considering offering in-home library service, as with any new library program or service, a good place to start is with agencies and individuals who work with seniors and persons with disabilities in your community, such as senior centers, city or county senior services, home health care workers, senior housing communities, Meals on Wheels, public transit services for seniors, the state office for social and health services, your churches, and any other community resources that you can think of in your area. This will not only create an opportunity for partnership and marketing your services in the future but will help you in your needs assessment. Having community partners in any endeavor is a tried and true method for success.

In "Homebound Services: Old Ways and New Ways," Gemmer also offers several suggestions for making your in-home library service successful. Sometimes in our efforts to cover all the bases, we overlook the most obvious, such as the following:

- Be sure that anyone who would be receiving books in the mail can get the packages delivered to his or her home.
- Make sure the books can be easily returned as well as easily received.
- Choose the right staff person or volunteer for the job. It should be someone who is congenial, social, and outgoing, and be sure to have a criminal background check on anyone doing home delivery.
- For moral support, you might send two people out on the initial visit.
- Have a budget for large print books and recorded books.
- Once a plan is developed and a budget to provide home library service is in place, identify clients through the community partners you've already engaged and through marketing.

Chelsea District Library

The Chelsea District Library (CDL) in Chelsea, Michigan, was awarded the 2008 Best Small Library in America, an award sponsored by *Library Journal* and the Bill & Melinda Gates Foundation. The annual award "was created in 2005 to encourage and showcase the exemplary work of libraries serving populations under 25,000. The winning library will receive a $15,000 cash award from the Gates Foundation, conference costs for two library representatives to attend the 2008 Public Library Association (PLA) meeting in Minneapolis, a gala reception at PLA, and more" (Berry, 2008).

CDL offers a number of programs to seniors and home delivery service, just two of the reasons CDL was given this prestigious award. CDL promotes home delivery service this way:

If you can't come to the library, let the library come to you! Those who cannot easily come to the library because of permanent or temporary illness or disability can elect to have books delivered to their homes.

Who is eligible?

You are eligible if you are a library district resident who is unable to visit the library due to permanent or temporary disability or illness. Upon entering the program, you will be issued a new "homebound" library ID.

Is there a fee?

Our service is free to eligible patrons. Also, there are no overdue fines, although you may be held responsible for lost or damaged items.

What materials can I borrow?

Books, excluding new books but including large print and paperback
Audiobooks on CD, cassette, or Playaway MP3 player
Magazines
Non-feature DVDs
Music CDs

How do I sign up?

Call us at (734) 475-8732 and ask for an adult services librarian. We will help you complete a homebound patron registration form that asks about the particular materials you would like delivered. You can also print the form as a Microsoft Word or PDF file and return it to us by mail or send an e-mail message to librarian Cathy Kamil or you may also call and leave a message for Cathy at 734-475-8732 ×401. After registration, we will set up a schedule for your home delivery.

Who will deliver the materials?

Materials will be delivered by trained volunteers or library staff.

How often will materials be delivered?

You will determine the frequency of delivery from one-time-only to monthly. All materials will be checked out to you for a four-week period.

Can I renew materials?

You may renew materials once, for an additional four-week period. However, renewals cannot be placed if someone else is waiting for an item.

How will materials be selected?

You will determine our level of involvement, which can range from filling specific title requests to regular staff selections based on your interest profile. Feel free to call us at any time with suggestions by title, author, subject, or genre.

How many items can I request?

> There is no limit. You may check out as many items as you expect to need for a four-week period. (Chelsea District Library, 2008)

Bill Harmer, head of Adult Services at CDL, suggests that in-home library service is "great PR for the library" and that libraries should be shameless in reminding their community of it. In his "Introduction to Senior Services" class at the Missouri State Library Summer Institute 2008, Harmer suggested the following ways to publicize your in-home library service:

- Create catchy flyers and place them at nursing homes, senior centers, hospitals, doctors offices, and residential facilities.
- Contact Meals on Wheels, churches, and synagogues.
- Work your already established contacts in the community.
- Promote the service on the library's Web site.
- Contact local newspapers to provide press for the service.
- Clearly state in all marketing that the service is free.

Harmer further suggested that librarians create paper and online applications, arrange visits in advance, and keep accurate files for your in-home patrons. Since in-home library service is different in so many ways from in-house library services, confidentiality of patron records is important but just a bit different. Serving as the reader's advisor for in-home library users does and should create a greater intimacy with the user's taste in reading or videos. Having this knowledge is useful to the staff person but should be regarded as strictly confidential. Keeping careful statistics and the shameless promotion of your service will serve you well in promoting the service to the library board, city council, or in doing presentations in your community.

The Right Person for the Job

In addition to good record keeping, finding the appropriate staff person or volunteer for in-home library service is crucial. The Australian Library and Information Association (ALIA) offers suggestions for ensuring that you have the right person for the job and that he or she is able to continue to do quality work in a position that can be emotionally and physically draining. They suggest the following:

- If used, volunteers should be screened, selected, trained, and orientated to their work by the home library service co-coordinator.
- Home library service work is physically and emotionally draining, home library service staff should not be involved in visits for more than four days per week.
- Two people should visit home library service users together, for reasons of occupational health and safety and security.

- Staffing levels should be determined from the number of users of the home library service, the frequency of visits, the level of service provided, the needs of patrons, and local conditions.
- In the absence of home library service staff, other adequately-trained library staff should be available to maintain continuity of service. (Australian Library and Information Association, 2000)

Skills Development

ALIA, also suggests that staff in the home library service area should have the opportunity to undertake internal or external training in areas such as:

- Interpersonal skills.
- Manual handling.
- Advanced driving skills.
- Aging awareness.
- Communicating with persons with disabilities.
- Stress management.
- First aid.
- Personal safety. (Australian Library and Information Association, 2000)

Security Issues

In-home library service providers also face security issues that many who work on-site do not face, and being away from the library premises or working alone can increase security risks. For this reason, personal safety training is recommended and some form of communication with the home library, such as a cell phones, two-way radios, or personal alarms should be available to in-home library service staff, for the protection of your staff and as a deterrent to any accusations of abuse.

On the Security Flip Side

"Millions more adults, both the elderly and individuals with disabilities who are in need of support, are served by numerous organizations and agencies. These encounters run the gamut from relatively brief interaction with a healthcare or recreation providers . . . to intensive dependent adult care services in or out of the home. The vast majority of these encounters are not harmful or abusive . . . abuses do, however, occur. Although studies are sketchy and do not provide a complete picture, one study indicated that 12.8 percent of the estimated 2 million incidents of elder abuse occurring in the home were perpetrated by service providers. A survey of 600 nursing home staff members suggested that elder abuse is a fact of institutional life: Of the staff surveyed, 10 percent admitted to physically abusing patients and 40 percent admitted to personally committing at least one psychologically abusive act in the preceding year. . . . Although the incidence of abuse may be relatively small, abuse traumatizes the victims and shakes public trust in care providers and organizations serving those most vulnerable" (Office of Juvenile Justice and Delinquency Prevention, 1998).

With the Violent Crime Control and Law Enforcement Act of 1994, Pub. L. No. 103-222, states could "authorize FBI criminal record checks of those working with individuals with disabilities or the elderly. In addition, the Attorney General was directed to 'develop guidelines for the adoption of appropriate safeguards by care providers and by States for protecting children, the elderly, or individuals with disabilities from abuse' and to 'address the availability, cost, timeliness, and effectiveness of criminal history background checks and recommend measures to ensure that fees for background checks do not discourage volunteers from participating in care programs.'" (Office of Juvenile Justice and Delinquency Prevention, 1998).

"The guidelines' main virtue lies in presenting a framework for making decisions about whom to screen and how. . . . The decisionmaking model begins with factors that trigger the need for screening, such as the level of direct worker-consumer contact, the characteristics of the consumer served, and the amount of worker supervision present. These triggering factors set the stage for determining the type(s) and extent of screening to perform. The next step is to consider the intervening factors that may limit the ability to perform certain kinds of screening, including cost, access, and time constraints" (Office of Juvenile Justice and Delinquency Prevention, 1998).

Most "organizations undertake at least basic screening, such as interview, verified application, and reference checks, even in those situations requiring the most cursory review. Thus, although some might suggest that no screening is necessary for situations in which the prospective volunteer or employee is known to the organization or agency, such an informal approach to screening is not advisable" (Office of Juvenile Justice and Delinquency Prevention, 1998). Organizations, including libraries, should develop "screening procedures and interview questions as part of their hiring or volunteer placement procedures" (Office of Juvenile Justice and Delinquency Prevention, 1998) and use them in all interviews. "Although screening to weed out potentially abusive individuals is important, it should supplement, not substitute for, an evaluation of skill development or competency. . . . All screening practices have limitations. Their use cannot guarantee that individuals who pass through the screening will not abuse children, the elderly, or individuals with disabilities in need of support. Thus, continuing to protect against abuse using posthiring screening and prevention procedures is warranted." (Office of Juvenile Justice and Delinquency Prevention, 1998).

Protection of Children, the Elderly, and Individuals with Disabilities

"The underlying reason for screening prospective workers who may come into contact with children, the elderly, or individuals with disabilities in need of support is the same: to identify potentially abusive individuals. When an individual entrusted with the care of someone abuses that person and then is found to have abused others previously, questions arise. How could such a person be in a position of caring for children or other vulnerable individuals? How can this be prevented from happening again?" (Office of Juvenile Justice and Delinquency Prevention, 1998).

The issue of screening volunteers and employees brings forth a number of questions: "How much screening should be done and who should decide? Should all who may or do come into contact with these vulnerable populations be screened? Volunteers versus employees? . . . What kind of screening should be done? Federal and State criminal checks? . . . Should a worker be 'on the job' in a paid or volunteer capacity pending the results of screening?" (Office of Juvenile Justice and Delinquency Prevention, 1998). The guidelines established by the attorney general in reference to the Violent Crime Control and Law Enforcement Act of 1994 provide background information for screening issues, affording those in a position to decide screening matters a solid base from which to make their decisions.

Pre-employment or Volunteer Screening

Most organizations can weed out potential abusive workers and volunteers by using standard interviewing and reference checking. However, there are "more complex and controversial procedures such as screening against child abuse, reviewing dependent adult abuse and sex offender registries, psychological testing, drug testing, and even home visits. (Not all of these practices can be undertaken in all States, however . . .)" (Office of Juvenile Justice and Delinquency Prevention, 1998). It is important to know the laws in your state. Here is a listing of some types of background screening mechanisms, ranging from the standard to the more rigorous:

Basic Screening Practices

- Employment reference checks.
- Personal reference checks.
- Personal interviews.
- Confirmation of education.
- Written application.
- On-the-job observation.

Frequently Used Practices

- Local criminal record check.
- State criminal record check.
- FBI criminal record check.

- State central child/dependent adult abuse registry check.
- State sex offender registry check.
- Nurse's aide registry record check.
- Motor vehicle record check.
- Professional disciplinary board background check.

Infrequently Used Practices

- Alcohol/drug testing.
- Psychological testing.
- Mental illness/psychiatric history check.
- Home visits. (Office of Juvenile Justice and Delinquency Prevention, 1998)

In looking at who should be screened prior to employment or volunteer service, we find a "multitude of settings in which abuse might be perpetrated. A partial list of settings in which individuals come into contact with children, the elderly, and individuals with disabilities gives a sense of the enormity of the contact points:

- Daycare: childcare, senior citizen centers, and community day programs for adults.
- Health/mental health care: hospitals, nursing homes/facilities, intermediate care, congregate care, board and care, group homes, psychiatric hospitals, residential treatment facilities, and "in-home" healthcare.
- Foster care: placements for adults in need of support services or for children under the care of the State as a result of abuse or neglect or as a consequence of delinquency.
- Other out-of-home settings: assisted living units/community living programs and semi-independent and independent living programs.
- Schools: public and private, including preschool and nursery school.
- Shelters: homeless or domestic violence shelters.
- Youth development: community or volunteer organizations serving youth.
- Volunteer programs (for the elderly or individuals with disabilities): Social Security representative payee, American Association of Retired Persons [AARP] bill payer and representative payee money management, Meals on Wheels, and other community/volunteer programs, [including in-home library service]. (Office of Juvenile Justice and Delinquency Prevention, 1998)

"In addition, criminal checks for home health aides were recently added to the Medicare requirements for home health agencies" (Office of Juvenile Justice and Delinquency Prevention, 1998). While we all want to feel that we know and trust those who work for and with us, taking a few extra moments to do a background check on a potential volunteer or employee who will go into the homes of older or dependent adults is a small price to pay for their security.

State Laws

"Legislation regarding the screening of persons working with children, the elderly, and individuals with disabilities has not been passed in all States . . . [and] most states do not maintain registries of persons who are being investigated for or who have committed abuse against the elderly or dependent adults. More than half the States have laws authorizing national criminal history checks for some type of person working with children, the elderly, or individuals with disabilities. A number of states also authorize state criminal history checks (either in lieu of or in addition to the national check). . . . Some states set forth a more expansive listing of crimes prohibiting employment, while others broaden their scope beyond the hiring of nurse's aides to all staff who have access to children and adults in need of supportive services—including, in certain circumstances, volunteers" (Office of Juvenile Justice and Delinquency Prevention, 1998). When sending workers into individuals' homes, it is important to consider the safety of the worker and the library user as well and to take proactive steps to ensure not only the quality of your in-home library service but the safety and security of everyone involved.

PROGRAMMING

In addition to services, such as in-home library service and lending libraries, programming can go a long way toward making those with disabilities feel that they are an important part of your library user community. If you aren't currently offering programs specifically for persons with disabilities, you might consider planning an activity, in conjunction with local agencies that already serve those with disabilities.

Art Abilities: Beauty in Differences

The Hennepin County Library in Minnesota offers a relatively simple project from the library's perspective but one that creates a very high-profile opportunity for outreach to persons with disabilities. Each year the Library hosts Art Abilities Gallery, "a celebration and exhibit of artwork by artists with physical and/or developmental disabilities" (Hennepin County Library, 2008). The Art Abilities Gallery project provides "an opportunity for area artists with disabilities to be part of a community art show to display their talents and skills. This art show focuses on abilities, not disabilities, and is an opportunity for people to express themselves in a creative way and contribute beauty to our community" (Hennepin County Library, 2008).

"The gallery is located in the library on the second floor and is open to the public free of charge" (Hennepin County Library, 2008). The exhibit includes a "pre-opening reception for the artists and their families, which also is open to the public and sponsored by the Library Foundation of Hennepin County. . . . Eight area non-profit organizations that provide services for persons with disabilities are collaborating with Hennepin County Library to present this exhibit in conjunction with National Disability Awareness Month" (Hennepin County Library, 2008).

This group of partnering organizations "invited some 4,200 Minnesotans with disabilities to create artwork for possible exhibition in the gallery. Hundreds of oil, acrylic, and watercolor paintings and photographs were submitted, and about 40 pieces are selected for display. . . . This is the fourth year that Hennepin County Library has exhibited the Art Abilities Gallery" (Hennepin County Library, 2008).

SHAKE THINGS UP: GAMING FOR ALL

In an article in the *Chicago Tribune,* "Disabled Gamers Want More Than 'Fluffy' Choices" (Gwinn, 2007), Eric Gwinn says that 10 to 20 percent of gamers are disabled in some way. The Accessibility Special Interest Group (ASIG) within the International Game Developers Association wants game makers to come up with more accessible games. In this article, they suggest that "programmers can help the visually impaired by letting gamers change color schemes and make letters larger, or output text to a Braille device. They can add closed captioning so that a deaf gamer and a hearing gamer can react to the same ambient sound—one gamer reads, 'The sound of footsteps from behind' while the other hears footsteps from behind" (Gwinn, 2007). At the present time, companies adapt their games for use by those with disabilities by adding mouth-controlled or other functions. With new technological advances every day, it seems that creating electronic games for people with all types of disabilities is possible.

In this article, we learn that not only are there disabled gamers out there but that many of them are unhappy with the types of games that gaming creators and manufacturers offer them. Gwinn suggests disabled gamers get little attention from the big game makers like Nintendo, Sony, and Microsoft. ASIG is trying to send a message to the gaming industry that most titles aimed at disabled gamers are too "fluffy," indicating a paternalistic attitude toward people with disabilities.

According to the article, members of ASIG feel that once prototypes are in place, it will be difficult for the big game manufacturers to deny it can be done, and to that end, Michelle Hinn, the head of ASIG and an instructor at the University of Illinois at Urbana-Champaign, "is organizing a game design seminar to build a socially oriented video game for players with quadriplegia. She hopes such hands-on design work will encourage gamemakers to keep the disabled in mind while creating their titles—and show them how" (Gwinn, 2007).

Some companies "have emerged to make custom adaptations for gamers with special physical requirements," (Gwinn, 2007) such as KY Enterprises. This "small Montana firm rewires controllers for the PlayStation 2 and Xbox 360, and then adds sip/puff straws and other controls. Called the KYE Quad Controller, the clunky metal device may not win design awards, but it lets gamers use their mouths to move characters on screen. The Quad Controller sells for $260 at http://www.quadcontrol.com" (Gwinn, 2007).

At http://www.accessibility.nl/games/index.php?pagefile=motoric we find information about the use of special controllers for video gamers. According to this Web site,

> many mainstream video games are more or less accessible for gamers with a physical disability, usually using special hardware. The most advanced hardware interfaces are mouth-controllers and head- or eye-trackers. Besides these controllers, alternative switch interfaces are used, which enable larger buttons or custom grouped buttons. Two good starting points for buying alternative game controllers are OneSwitch.org.uk and KY Enterprises. (Bartiméus Accessibility Foundation, 2006)

However, we also learn that while physically disabled gamers are able to use regular game controllers by honing their skills in order to play the game in a different manner, customizing controls for video games is still very important.

One-Switch or Retro Games

"For gamers with a severe physical disability, the number of controls might be limited to just one or two buttons. Some games are specifically designed to be played with just one button. These games are often referred to as 'one-switch'-games or 'single-switch'-games. Many early arcade games actually used only a few buttons but as games grew more complex, the number of controls increased. . . . For instance, the Playstation 2 controller consists of 15 buttons and two analog sticks. But with renewed interest for retro games and the rise of mobile games and digital television games, single switch gaming is gaining popularity. . . . The largest resource on gaming one switch games is Oneswitch.org.uk. The Retro Remakes website hold competitions with retro games. These retro games are often very suitable for people with physical disabilities since many use only one or two controls. Ablegamers.com is a website that looks to bring mainstream games to the disabled community. And you can discuss gaming with a physical handicap at the Game Accessibility forum" (Bartiméus Accessibility Foundation, 2006).

With the understanding that people with disabilities may be people who are interested in electronic gaming, librarians who are seeking ways to engage with those with disabilities in their own communities might consider some gaming activities as an attractive form of programming.

Wii-Habilitation

Some call it Wii-habilitation, but whatever the terminology you care to use, using the Nintendo Wii and other video games for people with temporary or permanent disabilities has become increasingly popular. Patients recovering from stroke or accidental injury in hospitals and clinics everywhere are rehabilitating with Wii Sports. In an article for MSNBC, Lindsay Tanner (Tanner, 2008) documents how, at Walter Reed Army Medical Center, Wii "therapy is well-suited to patients injured during combat in Iraq, who tend to be in the 19 to 25 age range—a group that's 'very into' playing video games" (Tanner, 2008). Many times patients view the activity as merely a fun activity, but physical therapists are able to see real improvement in movement and balance with users. Using the Wii adds variety and interest to the patients' rehabilitation process.

"The most popular Wii games in rehab involve sports—baseball, bowling, boxing, golf and tennis. Using the same arm swings required by those sports, players wave a wireless controller that directs the actions of animated athletes on the screen" (Tanner, 2008). Hospital spinal cord injury units are using the Wii to strengthen injured arms, fingers, and hands. Combining entertainment and therapy, patients improve endurance, strength, and coordination, according to the physical therapists interviewed in the article.

So, if physical therapists use Wii to increase movement and skills, why not use Wii in programming for people with disabilities that require wheelchair usage or whose motor skills might not be as finely tuned? Wii bowling requires minimal arm movement and very little arm strength. It is not only great fun but serves a purpose, and many people with disabilities are obviously interested in gaming. Be the first in your community to offer Wii bowling, or other suitable electronic games, to an underserved portion of the population.

OTHER SUGGESTIONS

The New Jersey State Library offers several examples of programs for persons with different types of disabilities; some are so surprising in their simplicity and usefulness that anyone can use and adapt them for their own library. Too often, library programming ideas fall into fixed categories of programming for children, programming for teens, programming for adults, and programming for seniors. Programming for those with disabilities spans all of these age groups, and it is possible that instead of providing additional programming, you might just need to ensure that all of your programs are accessible. If you want to add some additional programming, the New Jersey State Library offers these ideas:

- Develop programs that teach the use of the library, adaptive technology, online databases and the Internet which are specifically designed for persons with vision, hearing or learning disabilities. If applicable, provide the services of a sign language interpreter for persons who are deaf.
- Coordinate tutoring sessions at the library which link volunteers with persons with disabilities to provide training in: (1) use of adaptive technology; (2) use of Windows based synthetic speech screen reading programs for business

applications and searching the Internet; and (3) use of e-mail. If applicable, provide the services of a sign language interpreter for persons who are deaf.

- Develop a cooperative program with community and campus organizations, agencies, etc. that serve people with either vision, hearing or learning disabilities.
- Celebrate Deaf Awareness Week by: showing open captioned videos; demonstrating assistive devices (flashing light alarm clocks, a light signal doorbell and devices to warn parents when a baby is crying, etc.); teaching mini classes in sign language; presenting programs on deaf history and culture, etc.
- Sponsor a "Come Play with Us: Toys for Children with Special Needs" workshop presented in cooperation with a state Division of Developmental Disabilities.
- Present a workshop on parenting skills for parents of children with disabilities.
- Present programs for non-disabled parents of children with vision, hearing or learning disabilities and develop a collection of resource materials and a referral file or database for national, state and local organizations providing services for persons with disabilities.
- Present a program on adaptive telecommunications equipment, in cooperation with a local telephone company, which demonstrates how people with hearing, speech, vision or motor impairments can overcome problems in using a telephone.
- Coordinate basic reading and writing skills classes for adults who are deaf or have other disabilities.
- Develop a collection of tutoring materials, accessed by adaptive technology, for adults with vision, hearing and learning disabilities to improve their basic reading and writing skills.
- Present a program on living skills for people with disabilities.
- Offer beginning and intermediate courses in sign language which are free to library staff and people in the community. Courses may be taught by an interpreter or by a volunteer; and the library lends the textbooks to students.
- Sponsor a performance by [theater groups from schools for the deaf or blind] to be held at the library.
- Coordinate a talking book discussion group run by volunteers who lead the discussion.
- Coordinate the showing of captioned films for a monthly program of a local organization serving people who are deaf and/or hard-of-hearing.
- Present programs featuring educational or entertainment open captioned videos for persons who are deaf or hard-of-hearing and develop or expand a collection of circulating open captioned videos.
- Present programs featuring instructional, educational and entertainment American Sign Language (ASL) videos for persons who are deaf and develop a collection of circulating ASL videos and CD-ROMs.

- Present programs featuring educational or entertainment audio described videos which describe the action taking place for persons with low vision or who are blind and develop a collection of circulating audio described videos.
- Sponsor a Technology Awareness Workshop presented by a salesperson from a company that sells adaptive technology and invite blind consumers, resource teachers of visually handicapped, rehabilitation counselors, and employers to attend.
- Organize a vendors' fair at which company representatives show the latest modified and adaptive equipment, software and devices for helping people with disabilities in academic and vocation programs. Invite special education and vocational education teachers and administrators, parents and the community to attend the fair.
- Circulate kits for parents and deaf children that contain books, toys, a manual of suggestions for using the contents and a list or organizations to contact for further information. (New Jersey State Library, 1999)

And to ensure accessibility for individuals with hearing impairments in your regular library programming, you can:

- Arrange for library programs to be interpreted for deaf patrons when this service is requested.
- Equip a meeting room with assistive listening devices (ALDs) which are personal amplifiers that enhance volume and tone for hard-of-hearing people and invite community groups to use the facilities. Offer groups using the ALD equipped meeting room an orientation on the types of resources and services that the library can offer to persons who are hard-of-hearing. (New Jersey State Library, 1999)

CONCLUSION

Finding programs and services for those with disabilities in your community can be a rewarding experience. Think outside the box and plan gaming activities or offer up an opportunity to share artwork. Your efforts won't go unnoticed, and the rewards in providing services to an often ignored population will be many.

CHAPTER 3

Assistive Technology and Total Access

Just what is assistive technology and how can and do we use it in libraries? Assistive technology includes a wide variety of devices, both electronic and otherwise, used by individuals with disabilities in order to perform functions that they might not be able to do on their own. Assistive technology can be as simple as a wrist band that allows an individual to hold a pen or pencil, walkers and wheelchairs, and an ever-expanding arsenal of "hardware, software, and peripherals that assist people with disabilities in accessing computers or other information technologies" (Meredith College, 2009). The visually impaired often use software that reads text on the screen in a computer-generated voice, such as Job Access with Speech (JAWS), or people with low vision may use software that enlarges screen content, while people who are deaf may use a TTY (text telephone). Those with limited hand function may have a special keyboard or mouse to operate a computer. Assistive technology now encompasses a number of surprising devices that make life for persons with disabilities easier.

A legal definition of assistive technology was first published in the Technology-Related Assistance for Individuals with Disabilities Act of 1988 (the Tech Act). On June 23, 1988, Congressman Jim Jeffords of Vermont and Senator Tom Harkin of Iowa introduced this act, and on August 19, 1988, President Reagan signed the legislation. The act became Public Law 100-407. Persons with disabilities, their families, and advocates helped to define these issues as being crucial:

- People with disabilities and those involved with them, such as parents, siblings, friends, teachers, counselors, and employers, lack knowledge of and training in the use of technology and support services or the benefits that such technology and services would provide.
- Funding for technology and support services is uncoordinated, severely limited, and primarily dependent on a personal source of assistance or aggressive action by an individual to make it available from a nonpersonal source.
- There is no comprehensive system in place to help people with disabilities acquire technology, to ensure that such technology is appropriate or customized to meet an individual's unique needs or circumstances, or to provide training in, upgrading, replacement, or repair of such technology. (Morrissey & Silverstein, 1989)

The primary purpose of the Tech Act is to "assist states to develop comprehensive, consumer-responsive programs in technology-related assistance for disabled people of all ages and, thereby, overcome these serious problems" (Morrissey & Silverstein, 1989). This act was amended in 1994, and in 1998 it was repealed and replaced with the Assistive Technology Act of 1998.

THE ALLIANCE FOR TECHNOLOGY ACCESS

According to the Alliance for Technology Access (ATA) Web site:
Headquartered in Petaluma, California, the Alliance for Technology Access is a national network of:

- Assistive technology resource centers
- Individual and organizational associates
- Technology vendors and developers

The ATA is unique because:

- We were the first organization . . . and continue to be the only on of its kind in the nation that focuses solely on technology for people with disabilities, working on the national and local levels.
- We promote a consumer-directed service model.
- We recognize the changing need for technology over the course of a person's life, and therefore serve people of all ages and all disabilities.
- We work closely with technology companies to ensure the best and most accessible products possible. (ATA, n.d.)

Their mission "is to increase the use of technology by children and adults with disabilities and functional limitations.

The ATA is a growing national network of technology resource centers, organizations, individuals and companies. ATA encourages and facilitates the empowerment of people with disabilities to participate fully in their communities. Through public education, information and referral, capacity building in community organizations, and advocacy/policy efforts, the ATA enables millions of people to live, learn, work, define their futures, and achieve their dreams" (ATA, n.d.).

ATA supports over 40 local centers where persons with disabilities can get hands-on help and assistance with the tools. For a complete list of local centers visit http://www.ataccess.org/community/default.html.

So what does this mean for libraries? The ATA has some terrific tools on their Web site and also available by mail that can be adapted for use in your library. "Starting Points: Eliminating Barriers to People with Disabilities" (ATA, 2002), developed by Tom Morales, Russ Holland, Mary Lester, and June Kailes from 2002–2003, is one such tool. Funded by a grant from the Community Technology Foundation of California, "Starting Points" provides excellent self-assessment tools for community-based libraries, including your library. Publications such as "Starting Points" and other materials from the ATA can be obtained through the ATA Web site at http://www. ATAccess.org or by calling 707-778-3011.

In addition to "Starting Points" the ATA also offers "Access Aware: Extending Your Reach to Persons with Disabilities" (Morales, et al., 2001). The "Access Aware" manual "contains more detailed information to help community-based organizations move forward in their commitment to the process of acknowledging the presence of people with disabilities in their community and welcoming everyone to participate in their programs and services. The manual also provides guidelines, examples, ideas and resources to develop, implement and maintain an organizational Access Plan. This plan is an important step to assuring that an organization remains responsive to the needs of its entire community and provides people with disabilities the rights guaranteed by law" (ATA, 2002).

It is important to understand that access is not something that happens quickly or is accomplished all at once. Rather, access exists along a continuum and is a process that requires a sustained commitment. To be successful over time, it is important that your organization come to view increasing accessibility as part of their culture and core values. In order to initiate and sustain a process for increasing accessibility, ATA recommends that you take the following steps:

- Assign personnel to take responsibility for access. Include these duties as part of their written job description.
- Provide for staff development in this area.
- Commit to a written self-assessment, planning process, and development of a written 'Access Plan.'
- Review and update the Access Plan annually.
- Conduct outreach to persons with disabilities.

Access to community programs and services is a civil rights and social justice issue for people with disabilities. By establishing policies and practices that demonstrate your recognition of the rights of all people and your commitment inclusion, "you can have a dramatic effect on the lives of people with disabilities in your community!" (ATA, 2002). With self-assessment tools created by the ATA, you can easily identify achievable places to begin the process of making your library accessible to everyone, so why not start now?

COMMUNICATIONS

Before a person with a disability can make use of your library's programs and services, they have to be aware of your services and be able to effectively communicate with the library staff. It is your responsibility to provide the means to communicate with any individuals who want to use your library services and participate in the programs you have to offer.

Minimum Requirements for Effective Communication

Five items that are minimum requirements for effective communication are given in the following list, along with explanations for how further information can be located. In some cases, such as your provision of printed materials, the development is your responsibility.

1. Anyone who has vision, hearing, dexterity, speaking, learning or reading-related limitations, is able to communicate easily and effectively with your staff when seeking assistance.
   Example: Someone who is seeking information and is deaf could contact a staff member who is trained in the use of the telephone relay services. A description of the Telecommunications Relay Service can be found at: http://www.fcc.gov/cgb/dro/trs.html. A national directory of relay services can be found at: http://www.fcc.gov/cgb/dro/trsphonebk.html.
2. All people, regardless of ability, have full communication access while using your services.
   Example: Someone with a hearing loss could participate in a class that you offer with the assistance of a sign language interpreter or assistive listening device. Interpreters can be found by contacting the Registry of Interpreters for the Deaf, 301-608-0050, or your local Independent Living Center. [A directory of Independent Living Centers can be found at http://www.ilru.org/html/publications/directory/index.html. If you are unable to find a sign language interpreter in the directory, you might consider contacting a local public school or nearby college for someone who might have sign language knowledge and experience, without being certified, but you should try to locate the most highly qualified sign language interpreter that you can.]

3. Printed materials and information are available in accessible formats.
   Example: All materials can be produced in an electronic format that can be easily converted to Large Print or produced and distributed on CD.
4. Visual materials and information are available in accessible formats to meet individual needs.
   Example: Videos are captioned for people who are deaf or hard of hearing.
5. Public materials contain a statement that reflects your organization's accessibility policy.
   Example: Your brochure contains a statement such as "This organization welcomes people with disabilities. Our facility is accessible and within one block of the bus line. If you need any access accommodations such as a sign language interpreter or materials in an alternate format, please contact us five working days ahead of your visit and we will work with you to provide accessible services." (ATA, 2002)

The following is a communications self-assessment, created by the ATA and used here with permission from ATA. This self-assessment will help you determine if your library communicates effectively with persons with disabilities.

Communications: Self-Assessment

1. Does your organization do outreach to people with disabilities?   Yes _____ No _____
2. Does your organization maintain a list of sign language interpreters or interpreter services that you can contract with for services?   Yes _____ No _____
3. Does your organization provide captioning of the verbal content of its television public service announcements or videos?   Yes _____ No _____
4. Does your organization have written or other visual materials, such as videos, that it uses to provide information? This could include newsletters, brochures, applications, handbooks, etc.?   Yes _____ No _____
5. Do you have the text of the materials listed above in a simple, electronic text format? This means having material in a word processing program, such as MS Word, in a format without columns, tables, or other "complex" formatting?   Yes _____ No _____
6. Does your organization have more than one person trained in the use of the state relay system for people who are deaf or hard of hearing and/or Speech to Speech, the relay system for people with speech disabilities?   Yes _____ No _____
7. Choose your organization's four most popular written documents and indicate whether you have them available in the formats listed.

    7a. Item _____

Large Print	Yes _____	No _____
Computer disk or CD	Yes _____	No _____
Audio Tape	Yes _____	No _____

7b. Item _____

Large Print	Yes _____	No _____
Computer disk or CD	Yes _____	No _____
Audio Tape	Yes _____	No _____

7c. Item _____

Large Print	Yes _____	No _____
Computer disk or CD	Yes _____	No _____
Audio Tape	Yes _____	No _____

7d. Item _____

Large Print	Yes _____	No _____
Computer disk or CD	Yes _____	No _____
Audio Tape	Yes _____	No _____

8. Do each of the four documents contain an accessibility statement? Yes _____ No _____ (ATA, 2002)

Communications: Priorities and Next Steps

If you answered "No" to any of the questions, enter the problem areas in the chart.

Priority	Barrier	Solutions	Cost	Funding source	Due date	Responsible person

FACILITY

"In order for a person with a disability to make full use of the services and programs offered by your organization, they must be able to get to, enter, and navigate through your facility. Title III of the Americans with Disabilities Act requires that architectural barriers must be removed in public areas of existing facilities when their removal is readily achievable" (ATA, 2002). What is not readily achievable now may be achievable in the future, and it is important to recognize physical barriers to your facility and have a plan for removing those barriers. The ATA suggests the following as minimal standards of facility accessibility.

1. Everyone, regardless of mobility limitations, is able to independently enter, use, and exit your facility. Whenever possible, this means that everyone uses the typical entrance to your facility.
2. Everyone can travel freely through doorways and on pathways that are free of obstructions.
   Example: Someone using a wheelchair is able to use the paths of travel and pass through the doorways. This means that all of the doors should have handles (as opposed to knobs) that are no higher than 48 inches and can be operated with a closed fist. All doorways have a clear opening of at least 32 inches, and all travel paths are at least 36 inches wide.
3. Everyone has appropriate access to relevant resources and equipment.
   Example: If informational and/or training materials are displayed on racks and/or shelves, they must be no lower than 9 inches and no higher than 54 inches from the floor. There is also a 5 foot circle of unobstructed space in front of the display so that people using wheelchairs can turn around.
4. Everyone has access to areas where goods and services are provided.
   Example: There should be at least one computer workstation available on an adjustable height table. Everyone is able to get to and move around in any area where people routinely gather.
5. Everyone in your facility is able to get to and use conveniences that are available.
   Example: The restroom, drinking fountain, telephones, and other public conveniences are physically accessible. (ATA, 2002)

The following is a self-assessment, courtesy of the ATA, which will help you determine if your library is accessible to those in wheelchairs, with visual impairments, or other disabilities.

Facility: Self-Assessment

1. Can the public enter your facility without the use of stairs?   Yes _____ No _____

    1a. If you answered NO, do you have an ADA compliant ramp or other accessible method of entry?   Yes _____   No _____

2. Does the entry doorway have at least a 32 inch clear opening?   Yes _____ No _____

3. Are the routes of travel at least 36 inches wide?   Yes _____   No _____

    3a. Clear of obstructions?   Yes _____   No _____
    3b. Stable, firm, and slip-resistant?   Yes _____   No _____
    3c. If there are carpets or mats, are they less than 1/2 inch high?   Yes _____ No _____

4. Are door handles less than 48 inches high?   Yes _____   No _____

5. Are the tabletops and counters typically used by the public between 28 and 34 inches high, 30 inches wide and 19 inches deep?   Yes _____   No _____

6. Are there ramps, lifts or elevators to all areas that are used by the public?   Yes _____   No _____

7. Is at least one public restroom accessible?   Yes _____   No _____

    7a. Can the restroom and stall doors be opened with a closed fist inside and out?   Yes _____   No _____
    7b. Does the stall or restroom have an area of at least 5 feet by 5 feet, clear of the door swing?   Yes _____   No _____
    7c. Does the stall or restroom have grab bars behind and on the side wall nearest to the toilet?   Yes _____   No _____
    7d. Is the toilet seat 17 to 19 inches high?   Yes _____   No _____
    7e. Does one sink have a 30 inch wide by 48 inch deep clear space in front of it?   Yes _____   No _____
    7f. Is the sink less than 34 inches high?   Yes _____   No _____
    7g. Can the faucet be operated with one closed fist?   Yes _____   No _____
    7h. Can the soap dispensers and hand dryers be easily reached and operated with one closed fist?   Yes _____   No _____   (ATA, 2002)

Facility: Priorities and Next Steps

If you answered "No" to any of the questions, enter the problem areas in the chart.

Priority	Barrier	Solutions	Cost	Funding source	Due date	Responsible person

Accessibility to Library Services and Programs

As with its facility, a library's services and programs must be "accessible to people with disabilities in order for them to make full use of the opportunities that the organization provides. The processes of qualifying for, applying for and participating in your organization's services should be fair, equal and should not, even unintentionally, screen out people with disabilities" (ATA, 2002). The following are minimal steps toward accessible library services and programs:

1. The process of applying for and using your services is accessible for people with functional limitations.
   Example: You must offer someone with low or no vision assistance and/or an alternative to filling out an application. Accommodations and/or assistance are also available for someone who has difficulty reading English.
2. The criteria your organization establishes for participating in your programs is non-discriminatory.
   Example: If you require proof of identity to apply for your services, you must accept forms other than a driver's license. Because some people with disabilities, senior citizens and others with functional limitations cannot obtain a driver's license, they would be eliminated from eligibility if there were no allowance for alternate forms of identification.
3. Your services are offered in the most integrated setting possible.
   Example: If your organization offers a computer class, an accessible workstation is located in the same area as the rest of the computers. This provides equal access to the instructor, curriculum and peer support.
4. All of your public materials contain a statement that reflects your organization's commitment to providing reasonable accommodations for all of their programs, services and events.
   Example: Your brochure contains a statement such as, "This organization does not discriminate on the basis of disability in hiring or employment practices or in the admission to, access to, or operations of its programs, services or activities."
5. All public events sponsored by your organization, such as public meetings, fund-raising events, workshops are held in an accessible location.
6. The activities/content of all public events are accessible to people with disabilities.
   Example: People who are deaf or hard of hearing are able to benefit from a lecture through the use of interpreters or assistive listening devices. (ATA, 2002)

The following is a self-assessment for your library's programs and services, which will help you establish equitable policies for those with disabilities.

Services and Programs: Self-Assessment

1. Has your organization reviewed its written policies and procedures for all of its programs, services, and activities for practices that may be discriminatory toward people with disabilities or people who do not read and write in English? Yes _____ No _____

2. Does your organization assist people with disabilities or limited English skills in filling out forms it requires? Yes _____ No _____

3. Does your employee handbook/policy manual contain information about making reasonable modifications to policies or practices to ensure non-discrimination on the basis of disability? Yes _____ No _____

4. Do your materials that advertise your programs, services, and events contain a statement about your organization's commitment to non-discrimination and provision of reasonable accommodations? Yes _____ No _____

5. Does your organization have and use a guide for making sure all of your events and meetings, including off-site meetings, are accessible? Yes _____ No _____ (ATA, 2002)

Services and Programs: Priorities and Next Steps

If you answered "No" to any of the questions, enter the problem areas in the chart.

Priority	Barrier	Solutions	Cost	Funding source	Due date	Responsible person

TECHNOLOGY

An important portal to the information available in your library is through your online public access catalog (OPAC) and Internet access. It is critical that your "computers be flexible enough to meet the needs of a wide range of users, including people with vision, hearing, dexterity, learning, or reading-related limitations" (ATA, 2002).

Starting Goals

Starting goals for you to provide OPAC and Internet access are listed here:

1. The access features of the operating systems (OS) on all of your computers are installed.

   Example: Every computer has an operating system, the most common being Windows and Macintosh. Each of these systems has some built-in accessibility features that allow the user to adjust the keyboard, bypass the mouse, change the cursor, magnify what appears on the screen, and read text aloud. Information about the accessibility features of the Windows operating system can be found at: http://www.microsoft.com/enable/. Macintosh OS accessibility information can be found at: http://www.apple.com/accessibility/.

2. Staff and volunteers know how to activate, adjust and provide instruction on the accessibility features of their computers' operating systems.

3. At least one workstation, but preferably more, has assistive technology software programs that allow people who have vision, hearing, dexterity, learning, or reading-related limitations to perform basic functions on a computer such as word processing, e-mail and web "surfing."

   Example: Someone with limited English skills or a learning disability benefits from a word processor that gives audio feedback as they type and/or has a word prediction feature. A person with low vision could use a screen enlargement program. Someone with limited use of their hands can access the computer with a voice recognition system.

4. You have some basic assistive technology equipment that is available and maintained in good working order.

   Example: Your inventory could include, among other items, one or more mouse and keyboard alternatives and low tech aids such as a key guard or wrist supports.

5. Staff and volunteers know how to operate your assistive technology hardware and software.

6. Staff and volunteers know where to find information and resources about assistive technology hardware and software.

   Example: Develop and maintain a resource list that includes contact information for assistive technology resources for people with disabilities, such as:

- State Tech Act Programs—http://www.ataporg.org/atap/projects.php
- ATA resource centers—http://www.ataccess.org/resources/default.html
- ATA "Technology Toolbox"—http://www.ataccess.org/resources/atabook/

7. A line item that will provide for ongoing assistive technology purchases and upgrades is part of your technology budget. (ATA, 2002)

What follows is a technology self-assessment.

Technology: Self-Assessment

1. Do all of your computers have their operating system's accessibility features installed? Yes _____ No _____

2. Have your staff and volunteers been trained in the use of operating accessibility features? Yes _____ No _____

3. Is there a staff person who as part of their job description is responsible for the accessibility of your computers? Yes _____ No _____

4. Does your organization maintain a resource that lists contact information for assistive technology resources, such as ATA members or other assistive technology providers? Yes _____ No _____

5. Is there a written plan in place for the acquisition, upgrading, and maintenance of assistive technology hardware and software? Yes _____ No _____

6. Is there a written plan in place for staff training with new assistive technology? Yes _____ No _____

7. Does your organization have a way for computer users to notify staff of their accessibility needs? Yes _____ No _____

8. Does your technology inventory include some products from the following categories?

   8a. Keyboard Alternatives—Some computer users may have trouble using a standard keyboard because of dexterity or motor limitations. Do you offer alternatives to a standard keyboard such as a compact keyboard, large key keyboard, onscreen keyboard or voice recognition system? Yes _____ No _____

   8b. Mouse Alternatives—Because of functional limitations in the use of their hands, some computer users cannot use a standard mouse. Do you offer alternatives to a standard mouse such as a trackball, joystick or touchscreen? Yes _____ No _____

   8c. Enhanced View Monitor—Someone with low vision who needs to magnify what they see on the screen requires a larger monitor. Do you offer a [21 inches] or larger monitor? Yes _____ No _____

   8d. Voice Output Software—Someone who is blind or has difficulty reading English benefits by software programs that use synthesized speech to read aloud what appears on the screen. Do you offer software program(s) with voice output capability? Yes _____ No _____

8e. Low Tech Aids—There are many simple and inexpensive products that can make a computer more accessible for a wide variety of people. Do you have large print high contrast keyboard labels, wrist supports, keyguards or adjustable monitor mounts?   Yes _____   No _____   (ATA, 2002)

Technology: Priorities and Next Steps

If you answered "No" to any of the questions, enter the problem areas in the chart.

Priority	Barrier	Solutions	Cost	Funding source	Due date	Responsible person

Web Site

"Accessible web design can be a complex and highly technical field. There are, however, some very simple things that can be done to make a site very accessible. The World Wide Web Consortium (W3C) has the responsibility of developing standards for web accessibility through their Web Accessibility Initiative (WAI). WAI has developed a complete set of Web Content Accessibility Guidelines for web content developers that are divided into three priority levels, A, AA and AAA. It is compliance with these standards that you must meet in order to have a fully accessible web site. Attaining this level of compliance requires a sustained commitment of time and resources. When you bring your site into compliance with the Level A standards you will have made it accessible to a great number of people and will be well on your way" (ATA, 2002).

Starting Goals

Your starting goals for creating a Web site appear in the following list. The implication is that you have someone available to you to help you create this Web site. If your library has no one assigned to this task, perhaps another agency of government in your area will have someone to help you get started. It is important that you learn enough about this process that you can explain to someone helping you exactly what you want.

1. Your goal is to comply with the World Wide Web Consortium's Web Content Accessibility Guidelines 2.0 (WCAG 2.0). Take responsibility for the accessibility of your website even if you choose to outsource its design and maintenance.
   Example: Someone using a talking web browser, mobile phone or PDA, has full access to all of the information on your site because you have designed a site that provides text equivalents for graphic or audio information.
2. Your web person should be aware of the issues related to web accessibility and know where to find information, resources or expertise about them, such as:

   - Web Accessibility Initiative—http://www.w3.org/WAI/
   - WebAIM— http://www.webaim.org/
   - TPG—www.paciellogroup.com/solutions/development.htm

3. Your web person should be aware of the tools that are available to evaluate and improve the accessibility of web site content, such as:

   - A-Prompt—The Adaptive Technology Resource Centre at the University of Toronto—http://aprompt.snow.utoronto.ca
   - The Wave—WebAIM—http://wave.webaim.org
   - Evaluating Websites for Accessibility: Overview—www.w3.org/WAI/eval/Overview.html (Morales, et al., 2001)

Use the following Web self-assessment to get started on the road to Web accessibility.

Web: Self-Assessment

1. Have you assessed a sampling of your Web pages with the Wave?   Yes _____
   No _____
2. Are your web pages free of alt text errors?   Yes _____   No _____
3. Does the reading order of your Web pages make sense?   Yes _____   No _____
4. Are there functional equivalents for all applets?   Yes _____   No _____
5. Are your pages free of JavaScript or other accessibility errors?   Yes _____
   No _____

Web: Priorities and Next Steps

If you answered "No" to any of the questions, enter the problem areas in the chart.

Priority	Barrier	Solutions	Cost	Funding source	Due date	Responsible person

Testing for Web Accessibility

Does your library have a Web site? If it does, you'll be able to follow "How to Test a Web Site for Accessibility: A Step-by-Step Guide for Determining Whether Your Web Site is Accessible to Persons with Disabilities" (Satterfield, 2007). Brian Satterfield, staff writer for TechSoup, offers step-by-step guidelines for testing your Web site's accessibility. The article, with its easy to follow guidelines, is reprinted here with permission from CompuMentor.

Introduction to Web Accessibility

In May 1999, the World Wide Web Consortium (W3C) introduced its Web Content Accessibility Guidelines (WCAG) 1.0. The WCAG outlines steps that Web-site owners can take in order to make their sites usable by persons with disabilities such as low vision, color-blindness, and limited mobility. If a Web site fails to conform to the WCAG, a portion of your constituents and visitors may not be able to understand the site's content.

This tutorial explains how to test your Web site for a number of common, high-level accessibility problems. Section II describes six visual tests Webmasters can use to check their sites for accessibility and explains how to download, install, and use Job Access With Speech (JAWS), a screen reader used by visitors who are blind or partially sighted. Section III explains how to use and understand the Web Accessibility Versatile Evaluator (WAVE), a Web site that tests HTML code for accessibility errors.

While the testing tools used in this tutorial cost nothing, the following equipment and materials are necessary:

- A computer that runs Windows XP or 2000 operating systems with at least 200 MB of free hard-drive space. The computer should also have either audio outputs for connecting speakers or a headphone jack.
- Microsoft Internet Explorer version 6.0.
- Computer speakers or a pair of headphones.
- A means of documenting test results.

Note that while this tutorial explains how to perform accessibility testing, it does not cover methods to fix all detected problems. To fix detected accessibility problems, your organization should consult with a professional Web developer or conduct additional research.

Note 1: This tutorial provides instructions for accessibility testing using Internet Explorer. Mozilla Firefox users can also use this tutorial to test their sites, although some of the menu items will be different.

II. FRONT-END WEB ACCESSIBILITY TESTING

When testing a Web site for accessibility, start by checking the site's front-end elements, those items that users can see or hear. This section provides step-by-step instructions for performing six visual tests and one audio test.

A. Visual Accessibility Tests

To evaluate a Web site's content and design for accessibility, perform the following six visual tests.

Test #1: Ensure that link text is descriptive.

To ensure that links are meaningful to visitors who are using a screen-reading program, Web designers should make all link text as descriptive as possible. To do this:

Step 1. Open Internet Explorer.
Step 2. Enter the URL of the Web page you wish to test.
Step 3. Visually scan the site for links, which appear as underlined text, and read the sentences in which they appear. Example 1 demonstrates the type of language that fails to comply with accessibility guidelines, while Example 2 corrects the problem.

- Example 1: To learn more about Web accessibility, click here.
- Example 2: To learn more about Web accessibility, read the article "How to Test a Web Site For Accessibility."

Step 4. Repeat Steps 2 and 3 for each page on the Web site.

Test #2: Ensure that all images contain alt text.

Alternate text (often abbreviated "alt text") describes images or graphics on a Web page. To help visitors who are blind or have low vision understand which images appear on your Web page, ensure that all graphics contain alt text. To do this:

Step 1. Open Internet Explorer.
Step 2. Click the Tools menu item, located in the upper-left corner of the browser menu. A drop-down menu appears.
Step 3. From the drop-down menu, click the Internet Options menu item. A small window appears.
Step 4. Click the Advanced tab and scroll to the Multimedia subheading. Uncheck the box labeled Show Pictures.
Step 5. Close Internet Explorer and reopen it.
Step 6. Type the URL of the Web site you wish to test.
Step 7. Image placeholders will now appear in the place of actual images, along with alt text. Note any placeholders that do not contain alt text.
Step 8. Repeat Steps 6 and 7 for each page on the Web site.

Test #3: Ensure that text is readable at larger sizes.

Web surfers with low vision often set their Web browsers to display online text at larger sizes. To ensure that these visitors can read all site copy, enlarge text on a page to Larger and Largest sizes to check for inconsistencies or problems. To do this:

Step 1. Open Internet Explorer.
Step 2. Type the URL of the Web page you wish to test.

Step 3. Click the View menu item. A drop-down menu appears.

Step 4. From the drop-down menu, select the Text Size menu item. A small window appears, listing five text-size options.

Step 5. Click the Larger menu item. Scan the site to ensure that all text is readable and is not obscured by images or misaligned. Note any problems.

Step 6. Click the Largest menu item. Scan the site to ensure that all text is readable and is not obscured by images or misaligned. Note any problems.

Step 7. Repeat Steps 5 and 6 for each page on the Web site.

Test #4: Ensure that site does not scroll horizontally.

Visitors with limited mobility or ergonomic issues must be able to view a Web site with minimal movement. To ensure all text and images fit on the screen, check to see that the site scrolls vertically instead of horizontally. To do this:

Step 1. Open Internet Explorer.

Step 2. Type the URL of the Web page you wish to test.

Step 3. Look across the bottom of the browser window; no horizontal scrollbar should appear. If you see one, make a note of it.

Step 4. Resize the browser window by clicking the Maximize/Restore Down icon, located in the browser's extreme upper-right corner. (This icon looks like two boxes, one superimposed over the other.) Look across the bottom of the browser window; again, no horizontal scrollbar should appear. If you see one, make a note of it.

Step 5. Repeat Steps 3 and 4 for each page on the Web site.

Test #5: Ensure that site is navigable with keyboard.

Visitors with limited mobility or ergonomic issues may use the keyboard instead of a mouse to navigate a Web site. To ensure that all links and forms are accessible using a keyboard, try navigating the site using the Tab key. To do this:

Step 1. Open Internet Explorer.

Step 2. Enter the URL of the Web site you wish to test.

Step 3. Starting at the upper-left corner of the page, navigate the site using the keyboard's Tab key. Each time you press the Tab key, the browser should highlight a link or a form field. Navigate through the page with the Tab key, making sure that all forms and links are accessible in the proper sequence. Note any problems.

Step 4. Repeat Step 3 for each page on the Web site.

Test #6: Ensure that site has proper color contrast.

Visitors who are color-blind may not be able to view all colors on your site. To ensure that such visitors can view all text and images, test your site in grayscale (black-and-white) mode. To do this:

Step 1. Open Internet Explorer.

Step 2. Enter http://graybit.com/main.php into Internet Explorer's address bar. A Web page named GrayBit v1.0 appears.

Step 3. On the left side of the screen, the following text appears: GrayBit v1.0 Input Form Enter a Web Page URL. Immediately below it, a gray input form containing the text http:// accessites.org appears.
Delete this text and enter the URL of your organization's Web site.

Step 4. Click the button labeled Make It gray. Your site appears in grayscale in the browser window.

Step 5. Check to make sure that all text on your site is legible and that all images are visible. Note any problems.

Step 6. Repeat Steps 2 through 5 for each page on the Web site.

B. Audio Accessibility Test

To ensure that screen readers properly convey your Web site's text in audio form, test your site using Freedom Scientific's Job Access With Speech (JAWS), one of the most popular screen readers on the market. Note that while a full version of JAWS starts at $895, you can test audio accessibility of your Web site with the trial version, which lasts for six months and can only be used for 40 minutes at a time. Instructions for downloading the trial version of JAWS can be found at http://www.freedomscientific.com/downloads/demo/FS-demo-downloads.asp.

III. BACK-END WEB ACCESSIBILITY TESTING

After performing the front-end accessibility tests described in Section II of this document, test the site's HTML code to ensure there are no errors that could create accessibility problems. This section provides step-by-step instructions for using the WAVE accessibility tool to locate accessibility errors.

1. Submit the site to WAVE

To submit your site to WAVE:

Step 1. Open Internet Explorer.

Step 2. Type http://www.wave.webaim.org into Internet Explorer's address bar. The WAVE home page appears.

Step 3. Type the site's URL in the field labeled Enter the URL here. Click the Submit icon. Your site appears in the browser window.

Step 4. If your site now displays numbered symbols, save an HTML version of the page for later reference. Create a new folder on your computer's desktop by right-clicking anywhere, choosing New from the menu that appears, and clicking Folder. Name the folder WAVE_Tested_HTML_Files.

Step 5. In Internet Explorer, click the File menu item and select Save As. In the Save As window's left navigation area, click the Desktop icon and double-click the WAVE_Tested_HTML_files folder. In the Save As window's first drop-down menu, type the desired filename. From the second drop-down menu, select Web page, complete (*.htm, *.html). Click the Save icon.

Step 6. Repeat Steps 1 through 5 with all pages on your site.

2. Translate WAVE's error symbols

To translate WAVE's error symbols:

Step 1. Numbered symbols on a Web page submitted to WAVE indicate possible errors in the HTML code. These symbols can indicate that an HTML frame lacks a title. Therefore, the table will lack meaning to visitors who read the site's content using a screen reader or that the Web site contains a JavaScript-based form that automatically submits itself when a visitor selects an option from a drop-down menu. Since visitors who do not use a mouse may find this type of form difficult to use, you'll need to place a "Submit" icon next to the form.

Step 2. Enter http://www.wave.webaim.org/wave/explanation.htm into Internet Explorer's address bar to bring up the Index of WAVE icons page, which explains the meaning of all the error symbols. Note all detected errors.

IV. NEXT STEPS

The tests covered in this tutorial should help you detect high-level accessibility issues found on your organization's Web site. After completing these tests, contact a professional Web-development consultant or volunteer to help your organization fix the problems you find.

Once you fix the site's major accessibility problems, you may choose to delve a little deeper into the world of accessibility. To read the full text of the WCAG 1.0, open Internet Explorer and enter http://www.w3.org/TR/WCAG10/ into the address bar. (Satterfield, 2007)

If the idea of Web site testing seems formidable to you, invite one of your high school volunteers or employers or one of your avid users to test your Web site for you. Of course if, for whatever reason, you have not been able to create and maintain a Web site for your library, one of the pages or avid users may help you solve this dilemma, too!

Making your Web site accessible to everyone who visits the site increases your library's online reach, allowing for better service to persons with disabilities and the opportunity to attract new patrons, volunteers, and even potential donors.

A PRAGMATIC APPROACH

In "Access to Library Internet Services for Patrons with Disabilities: Pragmatic Considerations for Developers," Courtney Deines-Jones (1996) suggests that while most librarians would want to provide immediate access to all library Internet services, this might be beyond the reach of many libraries. Librarians must balance current patron needs with available resources, and then anticipate the needs of potential users. Deines-Jones lists some steps that serve as a general guide to making computer information accessible to the greatest number of people, without purchasing every adaptive aid on the market. She suggests that:

- Free material can be installed right away, and it should be advertised to bring in new patrons. As noted earlier, librarians can obtain many free programs from on-line sources. Vendors and associations that promote computer access for people with disabilities may also offer programs and, sometimes, equipment to libraries. State libraries may also have adaptive programs or equipment available upon request.
- Any purchases or serious programming commitments should be based on the demographics of the library's constituency. Special, school, and academic librarians can probably get information about patron disabilities from their personnel, admissions, and student affairs offices. Public libraries can probably get some demographic information from government and census information or from local disabilities advocacy organizations. Having this information ensures that any adaptive technology purchased or installed will meet the needs of actual users.
- People within the community must be involved in any plans to purchase or install equipment. If the library uses surveys to solicit ideas, they should be distributed to more than current patrons. Many people with disabilities could use the library, but do not know about adaptive interfaces or library services. Others may be unable to use present library services for some reason. Both groups represent important constituencies and must have a voice in any planning process.
- When the library does not have adaptive equipment available, librarians and other staff members must be willing to adopt work-arounds to help patrons. If, for example, there is no interface usable by a patron, a staff member can sit with the patron and type information based on the patron's dictation, reading the screen information back.
- If the library offers dial-in access or adaptive interfaces, these services should be promoted through venues likely to be seen by patrons with disabilities. For example, radio and television notices will reach more visually impaired patrons than will print advertisements, but radio advertisements will not reach most of the deaf community.
- Above all else, staff members must be willing to help. People with disabilities may need more time or assistance when they are using the system. If there are certain times of day that are quieter than others, patrons should know that at those times staff members can give them more one-on-one instruction.
- Both staff and patrons need training to navigate the Internet using adaptive equipment. A connection is useless if the patron does not know the types of information and services available on the Internet. Similarly, a staff member who knows the Internet well but who cannot use adaptive interfaces will not be much help to patrons. Consistent, ongoing training maximizes the effect of any equipment or software the library installs.
- Each library should designate one person to stay abreast of advances in adaptive equipment. (Deines-Jones, 1996)

COMMON ASSISTIVE TECHNOLOGIES
IN LIBRARIES

Hennepin County Library (in Minnesota) received a federal grant from the Administration on Aging and Centers for Medicare and Medicaid Services to improve access to information for older adults, persons with disabilities and caregivers. Their strategy was to place information in a variety of locations using a variety of formats. In keeping with these strategies, the library supplies a variety of assistive technology for library users, including:

- An adaptive technology lab, consisting of five workstations that feature 21-inch monitors and scanners. Software available for users with vision loss includes JAWS, Open Book Zoomtext Xtra, Kurzweil 3000 and Magic screen enlarger. The Adaptive Technology Lab also has devices for users with physical disabilities, including large keyboards, touchpads, trackballs and specialty mice.
- MAGic Pro is a magnification and speech program for low vision users. MAGic allows the user to magnify the screen up to 16 times the original size and "talks" to the user, repeating commands and helping to navigate the screen.
- JAWS for Windows is a screen reader. Designed for people who are blind, it allows users to access hyperlinks and content on a Web page. MAGic and JAWS are available at all suburban Hennepin County Libraries.
- Open Book is Optical Character Recognition (OCR) software which allows a user to scan mail, books, articles, or printed microform to an application which reads it.
- An electronic print magnifier magnifies any print item (may be handwritten) up to 45–60 times its original size and projects it on a TV screen.
- A hand-held magnifier enables people to enlarge and read print materials in the library. Available at the information desk at all libraries.
- POCKETALKER II is a personal microphone and headset system allowing individual amplification for the headset wearer.
- A television with telecaption decoder provides written captions of words as they are spoken on a television program that provides closed captioning (cc). Also accommodates closed captioned videos.
- An assistive listening system amplifies sound from a microphone through infrared system for persons wearing a headset and can be found in meeting rooms.
- The library also offers the option to reserve an item and have it sent to the most convenient library branch, as well as large print books, closed-captioned videos and DVDs, audio books, downloadable audio, and ebooks from NetLibrary and Overdrive. (Hennepin County Library, n.d.a)

THE ASSOCIATION OF ASSISTIVE TECHNOLOGY PROGRAMS

The Association of Assistive Technology Act Programs (ATAP) "is a national, member-based organization, comprised of state Assistive Technology Act Programs funded under the Assistive Technology Act (AT Act). ATAP was established in 1997 to provide support to state AT Program members to enhance the effectiveness of AT Programs on the state and local level, promote and formalize the collaboration of AT Programs with persons with disabilities, providers, industry, advocates, and others at the state and national level, and to increase the availability and utilization of accessible information technology (IT) and assistive technology devices and services for all individuals with disabilities in the United States and territories" (ATAP, n.d.).

At the ATAP Web site, http://www.ataporg.org/atap/projects.php?id=aboutus, you can locate your state's AT program and not only learn about it but also use this resource and refer patrons and caregivers to the program. If you are looking for programming or training on assistive technology, your state AT program will be a good resource for locating knowledgeable trainers or presenters.

CONCLUSION

Physical and intellectual access options are expanding as assistive technology in libraries becomes more commonplace, but library services will only be accessible to everyone if librarians make the effort to provide that access. Librarians should base assistive technology purchases on patron needs, and when assistive equipment is not available, they must develop workarounds or adaptive technology and be *willing to provide additional help to patrons.* Learning about your state's assistive technology program can not only benefit your patrons but serve as a resource for you and your staff, as well.

CHAPTER 4

Library Services to Baby Boomers and Older Adults

In 2006, the oldest of the Boomers, the generation born between 1946 and 1964, turned 60 years old. To commemorate the occasion, the U.S. Census Bureau newsroom compiled and released a collection of facts relating to the Baby Boom generation (U.S. Census Bureau, 2006). Here are just a few of the staggering statistics related to the aging Boomers:

- There were an estimated 78.2 million Baby Boomers as of July 1, 2005.
- There were 7,918 people turning 60 each day in 2006. That amounts to 330 every hour.
- About 50.8 percent of Baby Boomers in 2005 were women.
- In 1946, the estimated U.S. population was 141 million. Today, the nation's population stands at about 298 million. (U.S. Census Bureau, 2006)

Much has been written about this generation and aging, in reference to all sorts of issues from health and lifestyle to finance and work ethics. It stands to reason that if a substantial portion of the population is at a certain age and sharing in certain rites and passages of life as we know it, then that portion of the population might require a bit more attention from the local library. Courting Baby Boomers is a smart choice for many reasons that have been cited in numerous writings, a few of which we will reiterate here:

- Baby Boomers will likely be more active in retirement, as they were part of the generation of change and are determined to keep contributing and changing society, even as they age. The urge to keep contributing can make for a formidable volunteer workforce or library board.
- Baby Boomers are also likely to be seeking a second life or second career after retirement and might seek out information on career changes from their library.
- Baby Boomers are reluctant to grow old and will continue to experiment with new technologies and be interested in learning new things.

TRANSFORMING LIFE AFTER 50

The California State Library describes the 2007 Transforming Life After 50 Institute, funded by the Library Services and Technology Act (LSTA), as an effort at a statewide initiative

> to assist public libraries in redefining, creating and delivering new and innovative services to our state's growing population of active, older adults—a population expected to grow more than twice as fast as California's total population, increasing 112% from 1990 to 2020, or 8.5 million people. (California State Library, 2007)

A library field survey was undertaken in the fall of 2007 to assess current efforts to date in this regard.

The Transforming Life After 50 Institute was designed to promote an "understanding of how the size, history and significance of the Boomer cohort, along with their extended life spans, will impact aging in America" (California State Library, 2007). Emphasis was given to the importance of viewing these older adults as resources for their communities. Partnerships with Libraries for the Future and the California Library Association were undertaken to leverage resources and broaden perspectives. The resulting three-day training institute in November 2007 was attended by 88 participants, representing 44 California library jurisdictions.

Presentations were given from leaders in the fields of health, education, social science, anthropology, spirituality, and aging, and these video presentations from the institute were available online at the time of this writing at http://transforminglifeafter 50.org/, and included such presentations as "Lifelong Access: A Vision for Public Libraries," by Diantha Schull (2007), "Boomers Health Care and Economic Security: It Isn't One Size Fits All," by Ernie Powell (2007), "Building Health in Our Communities," by Richard Jackson (2007), and "How Libraries Can Respond," by Matt Thornhill (2007).

In his presentation, Thornhill suggests that in order to engage Boomers, librarians should:

- Talk to Boomers in your community when developing programs for them.
- Engage partners to increase visibility of your programs.
- Avoid the word "seniors" (although the word "senior" itself suggests someone who has achieved a certain status in life through experience and wisdom—such as senior partner in a law firm).
- Get to know your local volunteer matching organizations.
- Develop programs with an audience in mind, but under major themes, such as health, finances, career, and volunteerism.

Thornhill also suggests some specific program ideas, such as "Mastering Being a Caregiver," "Encore Careers," "Dating at Any Age," and "New Grandparents Rules and Regulations."

In looking at these suggested programs, it reminds us that the Baby Boomers are the sandwich generation, taking care of elderly parents while juggling grandbabies on their knees. Without special attention to this portion of the population, you might miss out on their presence in your library.

REALITIES

In light of the senior boom and the particular characteristics associated with this demographic, libraries everywhere have taken on the challenge of offering innovative programs and services to older adults. While senior Boomers may not go as quietly into the night as their fathers before them, they will nevertheless have to deal with the reality of aging. How can we be so sure of this simple fact? We are Boomers too, and we don't hear as well as we used to, and the eyesight suffers just a bit, in spite of the relatively trim waistlines and toned calves. The times are a-changing, and we are a-changing too.

The Physical Changes

A myriad of things change as we get older when the hair starts to gray, the waistline expands, and the joints and muscles ache. Other changes affect the way we learn as we age. According to an article by Carol Bean (n.d.), Library Computer Center Manager of the North County Regional Library, Palm Beach County Library System, and creator of Mousing Around, there are several factors that can affect the way older adults learn:

1. Arthritis
2. Tremors
3. Vision
4. Cataracts

5. Hearing
6. Increased distractibility
7. Neural noise
8. Slower cognitive processing
9. Conceptual knowledge
10. World knowledge
11. Automatic processes
12. Language
13. Health
14. Motivation and psychological factors (Bean, n.d.)

While not every older adult is affected by any or all of these factors, chances are that as we grow older, we may all be affected by some of them. In a preconference workshop at the 2007 American Library Association (ALA) Conference in Washington, DC, Bean did a wonderful job of illustrating how distractions online (Who isn't mesmerized by the dancing figures advertising falling mortgage rates on Weather.com?), simple tinnitus or more serious hearing loss, and arthritis can all affect how older adults are able to function and learn in a computer technology training session. Bean used examples of how word associations or words that mean something else to an older person, such as icon, scroll, browser, and drive, can serve as a distraction in a computer class, as well as examples of activities that mimic computer work—like tapping one's fingers in a specific pattern while reading words on a screen, or trying to write a word in a foreign language with the nondominant hand while viewing random images—to illustrate how challenging learning to use a computer can be for those of us who did not grow up in the computer age.

GUIDELINES FOR LIBRARY AND INFORMATION SERVICES TO OLDER ADULTS

The Reference Services Section of Reference and User Services Association (RUSA) of the American Library Association approved *Guidelines for Library and Information Services to Older Adults* in June 2008. The "updating of these guidelines began in 2005. Current and past members of the Committee on Library Service to an Aging Population and the Office of Literacy and Outreach Services (OLOS) Library Service to the Aging Subcommittee contributed to this revision" (RUSA, 2008). Section 3 of the guidelines addresses some of the issues involved in making the library more accessible and welcoming to older adults who might be experiencing some changes.

- Make the library's collections and physical facilities safe, comfortable and inviting for all older adults.
- Evaluate your library's accessibility by older adults with physical, visual, aural, reading and other disabilities, according to the Accessibility Guidelines for Buildings and Facilities of the Americans with Disabilities Act.

- Consider providing at least one wheelchair in the library for public use.
- Accommodate users for whom prolonged standing is difficult by placing chairs or stools near stacks, information desks, check-out areas, computer terminals, and other areas. If possible, create a "Senior Space," using easy chairs gathered in an area adjacent to books and magazines of interest to older adults.
- Consider placing materials frequently used by older adults on easily accessible shelves.
- Place paperbacks, clearly labeled and well spaced, in areas of the library that are especially well lit, accommodating older adults who prefer paperbacks over heavier and more cumbersome hardback books.
- Assure that spacing between shelving accommodates users in wheelchairs.
- Ensure that signage is clear, Brailled (where appropriate), and readily visible to all, including users in wheelchairs. Library brochures should be in at least 14-point font type.
- Provide at least one computer station prominently labeled and installed with large type software for older adults with low-vision. If needs warrant and resources are available, acquire other assistive technology such as a stand-alone Reading Machine which speaks the book's text to a blind reader; speech synthesizer and related software; low-tech magnification and other devices.
- Provide TTY access, closed-captioned videotapes, and assistive listening systems to older adults with hearing disabilities.
- Acquire and make available books and periodicals in large print. (RUSA, 2008)

To view the guidelines in their entirety, visit: http://www.ala.org/ala/mgrps/divs/rusa/resources/guidelines/libraryservices.cfm.

In the National Council on Aging's (2008) public policy update, "State Aging Programs Hit by Economy," we find that 67 percent of states say their aging programs are experiencing a budget shortfall, and 14 states report this is at least the second consecutive year of cuts, according to a new survey by the National Association of State Units on Aging (NASUA).

At the same time, because of the aging Baby Boomers, the demand for assistance continues to rise, according to the 44 states that participated in this survey, along with the District of Columbia. More than 60 percent of respondents reported increases in requests for home-delivered meals, transportation, and home heating. While all states reported proposed cuts in program administrative costs, over 80 percent said they have seen an increase in calls seeking general information and referral to the aging network. Nearly 70 percent are anticipating cuts in programs for older Americans and the disabled. While libraries cannot fill in the gap for Meals on Wheels, there are many ways that libraries can partner with other local service agencies to provide services and enhance the quality of life for older adults and those with disabilities.

Computer Training for Older Adults

Many libraries now offer computer classes strictly for older adults, and it's a good thing too. Without the assistance of library computer classes everywhere, many seniors living on fixed incomes would end up paying for computer training at the local community college or computer store or would not have the training at all. Older adults, like everyone else, increasingly find it necessary or desirable to be able to use computers. Many enjoy the ability to have instant communication with their families and especially their grandchildren as well as to check bank accounts and even buy products online.

The Pew Internet and American Life Report indicates that seniors 65 and older using the Internet have increased in the last five years from 22 percent to 35 percent, and it has been suggested that local library computer training classes for seniors might be responsible for the increase, although this statement has not been substantiated.

In "Adapting to Seniors: Computer Training for Older Adults" (Bean & Laven, 2003) Carol Bean and Michael Laven of the Palm Beach County Library System (PBCLS) describe how this system "opened a computer lab in its North County Regional Library (NCRL) to offer computer classes to the public. Like other libraries in the area and across the nation, we focused on classes teaching the basics of Microsoft Windows, using a browser, and simple word processing. Demographically, the area has a high percentage of retirees, so it was not surprising that the vast majority of class participants have been from the older generation" (Bean & Laven, 2003).

As they began teaching classes at the NCRL, they quickly discovered the older generation often had a harder time mastering basic computer skills and grasping some of the basic concepts. They learned that older adults can learn to use computers, and even become expert users, but because of changes that occur with aging, they require a different instructional approach. Older adults need the following:

- Much more repetition and practice for new skills to become automatic. Consequently it is necessary to take time to repeat tasks throughout the lesson to reinforce new skills and concepts and include optional practice times to each class, with exercises to review what was covered in class.
- A modification of the terms we use to introduce new concepts, to prevent unwanted word associations. They suggest you introduce icons, for example, by referring to them first as pictures and to connect terms like "shortcut" and "menu" with an explanation that associates them with the new meaning.
- Modified handouts to make them more senior-friendly with simple, step-by-step instructions using clear, concise, wording, in an easy to read font and size such as Helvetica and Arial and abundant, labeled graphic illustrations to keep their attention focused.
- Assistance with choosing classes appropriate for their level of skill. To avoid the problems inherent in teaching novices and more experienced computer users, place people in classes that suit their skill level. Have the reference staff

who register patrons for classes periodically assist with classes so they can be aware of the experience level needed for each class.

According to the article, the trainers at NCRL found that older novices needed more repetition and a slower pace, with a practical application of the skills they had learned. These trainers developed classes for older adults with several key differences from other classes:

- They insist on out-of-class assignments, which must be completed before the next class, to aid in repetition and retention.
- They offer two classes a week so that there is less time to forget what was learned, especially when the assignment is done at least once before the next class.
- They require a commitment to four classes and doing all of the assignments before they sign up for the course.
- Only class instructors can register patrons for this class to make sure that the participants get into the right class.

Selecting prospective students created a problem for the trainers. "We initially did not advertise the classes, or even list them on our monthly calendar of classes, opting instead to identify possible students in the sign up process. Since we started listing the classes on our monthly calendar, we have had many more people requesting the class than actually need it, despite class descriptions which make it clear the class is not for everyone. We have found we still must go through an interesting Reference Interview process to weed out the ones who would do better with the regular classes. For example, a typical series of questions we use to determine the experience level, motivation, and age-related issues which the slower classes specifically address are:

- Do you have a computer?
- Do you use any of the computers at the library?
- What are some things you do with the computer? (or What is something you tried to do with the computer?)
- What do you want to do with the computer?

Their answers to these questions give us a much better indication of their experience level, abilities, and motivation than simply asking, 'Do you know how to use a computer?' For instance, if they are successfully sending and receiving e-mail on a computer, they do not need either the Mousing class or our Getting Started series of classes" (Bean & Laven, 2003).

In these computer classes, the methods of introducing the various components of computer use are well established and successful. The trainers recommend that the first class, called Mousing Around, should be devoted to learning about the computer mouse. You can find Mousing Around at http://www.pbclibrary.org/mousing/. In keeping with their policies, they require the students to come back to the library and do the Mousercising practice again before the next class.

In the second class they, of course, "review what they need to know from the first class, and then teach them how to open and close the browser, how to enter a URL, and how to use the back and forward buttons" (Bean & Laven, 2003). The assignment after the second class is to "sign up for an Internet terminal on their own, open the browser, and play one of the games on the Games page of [the] Mousing Around tutorial" (Bean & Laven, 2003).

In the third and fourth classes, "the students sign up for a free web-based e-mail account and learn how to send and read e-mail, how to delete old messages, and empty the 'trash.' Their third assignment is to send e-mail messages to two library accounts which are set up to auto-respond, so they will have messages in their inbox to read when they get to the last class" (Bean & Laven, 2003).

Class "handouts for this series make heavy use of graphics and use simple, clear language. The assignment instructions are in a step-by-step format, also with extensive, labeled graphics" (Bean & Laven, 2003).

If you are considering setting up computer classes for older adults in your library, you couldn't go wrong with the tried and true methods of Carol Bean and the trainers at the NCRL.

Older Adults and Web 2.0

Offering basic computer courses geared specifically to older adults is nothing new, although there are still libraries that haven't found the time or that lack the staff to offer such courses. To librarians in those libraries, we want to encourage you to look for a patient volunteer to train some of your older adults. Finding the right teen or group of teens in your community to provide computer classes for your older patrons would make an excellent intergenerational activity in your library. Remember: the kids are learning it in school, but the older folks don't have that luxury. Sometimes the public library is the only place that those of us who didn't grow up using computers can find computer training.

But what about going beyond the basics of computer usage? What about the Web 2.0 applications for older adults? What about social networking and online gaming? Why should the kids get to have all the fun? Libraries from coast to coast are incorporating electronic gaming and making use of social networking applications in their programs for seniors.

At the Old Bridge Public Library in Old Bridge, New Jersey, former assistant director and head of public services, Allan Kleiman, created a "Senior Space" through an LSTA grant from the New Jersey State Library and the Institute for Museum and Library Services. In a series of "Libraries, Older Adults, and Web 2.0" workshops held in Missouri in October of 2008, Kleiman suggested to participants that they take the programming that they are currently doing with seniors and then try to think of ways to add Web 2.0 applications. So, for example, if you offer a monthly program for seniors and once a year you focus on music, why not use YouTube to find excerpts from Broadway musicals, opera, or choral performances and create a program that way? If you already have a book discussion club, create a blog around the discussion, or offer electronic gaming as a senior activity. Kleiman asked workshop participants in Missouri, "If we don't show our seniors about social networking or Web 2.0, who will?" (Kleiman, 2008).

Senior-Friendly Web Sites

In "Making Your Web Site Senior Friendly," the National Institute on Aging and the National Libraries of Medicine (2001) have created a checklist for Web designers that can help open the Internet to great numbers of people over 60 who want to know more about their health and aging (http://www.nlm.nih.gov/pubs/checklist.pdf). "While advanced age is not a hindrance to computer or Internet use, there are normal, gradual age-associated declines in vision and certain cognitive abilities that may limit the use of electronic technology" (National Institute on Aging and the National Libraries of Medicine, 2001). The checklist offers several suggestions that will make your Web site more accessible to older adults with declining vision. Following the guidelines will improve readability of online text. First of all they suggest that you do the following:

- Use a sans serif typeface [a typeface that does not use serifs, small lines at the ends of characters], such as Helvetica, that is not condensed. [Sans serif typefaces include Helvetica, Arial, Univers, and News Gothic.] Avoid serif typefaces like Times New Roman, and novelty typefaces like Old English Text and Bodoni Poster.
- Use 12 point or 14 point type size for body text.
- Use medium or bold face type.
- Present body text in upper and lowercase letters. Use all capital letters and italics in headlines only. Reserve underlining for links.
- Double space all body text.
- Left justified text is optimal for older adults.
- Avoid yellow and blue and green in close proximity. These colors and juxtapositions are difficult for some older adults to discriminate. Ensure that text and graphics are understandable when viewed on a black and white monitor.
- Use dark type or graphics against a light background, or white lettering on a black or dark-colored background. Avoid patterned backgrounds.
- Present information in a clear and familiar way to reduce the number of inferences that must be made. Use positive statements.
- Use the active voice.
- Write the text in simple language. Provide an online glossary of technical terms.
- Organize the content in a standard format. Break lengthy documents into short sections.
- Use text-relevant images only.

- Provide text alternatives such as open-captioning or access to a static version of the text for all animation, video, and audio.
- The organization of the web site should be simple and straightforward. Use explicit step-by-step navigation procedures whenever possible to ensure that people understand what follows next. Carefully label links.
- Use single mouse clicks to access information.
- Use a standard page design and the same symbols and icons throughout. Use the same set of navigation buttons in the same place on each page to move from one web page or section of the web site to another. Label each page in the same location with the name of the web site.
- Incorporate text with the icon if possible, and use large buttons that do not require precise mouse movements for activation.
- Avoid automatically scrolling text. If manual scrolling is required, incorporate specific scrolling icons on each page.
- Incorporate buttons such as "Previous Page" and "Next Page" to allow the reader to review or move forward.
- Provide a site map to show how the site is organized.
- Use icons with text as hyperlinks.
- Offer a telephone number for those who would prefer to talk to a person [or provide an e-mail address for questions or comments].
- Solicit unbiased comments from older adults through focus groups, usability testing, or other means to evaluate the accessibility and friendliness of the web site. (National Institute on Aging and the National Libraries of Medicine, 2001)

For an example of a senior-friendly Web site that was developed in accordance with these guidelines, log on to http://www.nihseniorhealth.gov. This Web site was jointly developed by the National Institute on Aging and the National Library of Medicine.

Many libraries have Web pages or sites dedicated to their older adults. The Wilton Library in Wilton, Connecticut, has a Web site devoted to their seniors at http://www.wiltonlibrary.org/senior, listing many resources for older adults in their community. In Traverse City, Michigan, the Senior Corner site at the Traverse Area District Library is an award-winning site, which includes not only articles and information of local interest but also computer tutorials, free downloads, and numerous links to other resources. This Web site boasts including "national and international resources which focus on seniors and their needs. You'll find easy connections to huge amounts of information: federal agencies, consumer groups, senior e-zines, physical and mental health websites, grief resources, amusing and instructive diversions, and much more. There's also a nifty search engine if you don't find what you're looking for" (Traverse Area District Library, n.d.).

Blogs

The Old Bridge Public Library, where Allan Kleiman did so much of his work, has a Web page devoted just to their older patrons. This page includes a listing of programs for seniors, online newspapers and databases that seniors might use, and a blog. A blog is an easy way to allow older adults to share their writings online—even if you have to post the writings yourself. On the Old Bridge Public Library senior blog, you will find writings by library staff and patrons alike at http://seniorspaces. blogspot.com.

Seniors and blogs are a natural fit. In *The Mature Mind: The Positive Power of the Aging Brain*, Dr. Gene Cohen (2006) discusses the "summing up" (p. 75) phase that older adults experience, in which they identify with being "keepers of the culture" (p. 76) and often express themselves creatively through storytelling, memoirs, oral histories, and family genealogies. If you have a group of seniors that are already participating in oral history projects, poetry, or other types of writing activities, why not set up a blog for them? At http://jenett.org/ageless, the Ageless Project demonstrates that blogging is for all ages. At the Ageless Project, we find 3 bloggers represented there that were born before 1920, 21 born in the 1920s, and 49 born in the 1930s. By creating a blog for your seniors, even those who use in-home library service, you can create an online community for them to share their life's experiences, poetry, book reviews, or other writings.

Gaming . . . Again

If your particular seniors are less introspective and more competitive in nature, why not encourage them to participate in gaming activities? Much can be said about the benefits of all sorts of gaming, both high-tech and not-so-high-tech. From simple crossword puzzles to electronic and computer challenges, everyone is touting the brainpower-boosting capabilities of games. According to the Franklin Institute (2004), "Numerous studies show that better-educated people have less risk of Alzheimer's disease. In a Case Western Reserve study of 550 people, those more mentally and physically active in middle-age were three times less likely to later [develop Alzheimer's]."

"Increased intellectual activity during adulthood was especially protective. Examples included reading, doing puzzles, playing a musical instrument, painting, woodworking, playing cards or board games, and performing home repairs" (Franklin Institute, 2004). The Franklin Institute Web site offers numerous suggestions for keeping the brain active and increasing cognitive skills, for groups and individuals as well. Something as simple as using the nondominant hand to eat or brush your teeth strengthens neural connections. The Franklin Institute even suggests that older adults who play bingo have better cognitive function. Who knew? Providing our seniors the opportunity to participate in group games in the library is just one more way libraries keep us on our lifelong learning path.

Puzzles such as Sudoku, logic problems, crossword puzzles, and riddles for individual use are available in the magazine section at most stores. For group activities, however, there are a variety of games that you can host for seniors in your library. Why not have a checkers or chess tournament or use one of the numerous word-based games that are available on the market to create a fun learning experience in the library? "Just as exercising your body improves your physical form, solving crosswords, Sudoku, logic puzzles and computer mental fitness games improves your mind and increases your brain cells. Although puzzle solving has been popular for years, the technology of improving the brain with online puzzle websites and computer brain-enhancement programs has gained an edge" (Carrier, 2008).

In addition to electronic games, the printed puzzle is still a great option for exercising the brain. Its portability and the sense of satisfaction upon completion that it conveys is unbeatable for many puzzle fanatics. Various puzzles available that you can do are Sudoku, logic problems, crossword puzzles, riddles, and Quotefalls. For group activities in the library, there are a variety of board games that you can do as well, such as checkers, chess, Scattergories, Cranium, Boggle, and Balderdash, just to name a few. Playing games is a great way to stimulate the brain and develop critical thinking skills.

Studies now show that brain-training exercises have lasting effects, especially for the elderly. According to *The Mature Mind: The Power of Older Minds* (Cohen, 2006, p. 24), "The brain is like a muscle. Use it, and it grows stronger, but let it idle, and it'll grow flabby." In this excellent book on aging and the mind, Cohen tells us that engaging in new learning experiences boosts the development of the brain by generating new synapses and other neural structures in the brain. While it has long been known that regular physical exercise can improve and maintain your health, research into the area of brain fitness is more recent, and studies indicate that performing mental exercises on a regular basis can help to improve and maintain common brain functions, such as memory and problem-solving skills. According to the Franklin Institute (2004), "Severe mental decline is usually caused by disease, whereas most age-related losses in memory or motor skills simply result from inactivity and a lack of mental exercise and stimulation." Choose from any number of activities you can do to keep older minds active in your library. It can be challenging yet enjoyable.

Electronic Games

What about all those video games that boast brain stimulation and improvement in hand-eye coordination? There are numerous Web sites that your seniors can visit to play games online. For example, Eons, a Web site specifically for older adults, has online games that you can play for free. You can introduce your seniors to Eons at http://www.eons.com. The games on this and other Web sites can be played by an individual or in an online group environment, offering gaming competition at home or in the library. Pogo, for example, has a large selection of single and multiplayer card, board, and word games for free at http://www.pogo.com.

Video games such as Big Brain Academy for the Nintendo DS and Wii systems are extremely popular with all age groups. According to Kathy Carrier, in "Games Offer Brain Workouts" (Carrier, 2008), electronic and computer game sales have climbed from $70 million in 2003 to an estimated $225 million in 2007, in the United

States. The brain game market has grown by leaps and bounds in a period of a few years, in part because of the senior boom, and if electronic and computer game sales are any indication, the world should be getting a whole lot smarter.

Electronic Brain Games

Here are a few popular choices for the best brain games:

- Brain Fitness Program: Only commercial software backed up by research suggesting it enhances brain function. Users wear headphones and use a computer to perform audio exercises.
- MindFit: PC software offering exercises to improve short-term memory, reaction time, eye-hand coordination, and more. Tracks performance over time.
- Brain Age: Inspired by the research of a Japanese neuroscientist. Nintendo's handheld DS system includes 15 puzzles and exercises, plus 100 Sudoku puzzles.
- Big Brain Academy: For Nintendo's Wii or DS hand-held systems. Up to eight players compete in myriad activities, from memorization to math problems.
- My Brain Trainer: Website offering 39 exercises.
- Radica Brain Games and Brain Games 2: Mattel's hand-held games feature exercises that ask you to complete sequences, find hidden words and more. (Carrier, 2008)

According to the article by Carrier, Alvaro Fernandez, chief executive and cofounder of SharpBrains.com, says that "The more you use your brain, the better it's going to function. Two years ago, no one understood brain training, and that the brain continues to form new connections when stimulated in the right ways" (Carrier, 2008). Not all electronic games are suitable for group activity, and you will have to experiment to find out what works in your library.

We Like to Play . . . Wii

It's a fact. Libraries from coast to coast are offering Nintendo Wii for young and old alike. It started with just a few—Allan Kleiman at the Old Bridge Public Library was one of the first—but now libraries everywhere are getting in on the Wii video game action. Wii Sports, particularly bowling, seem to be the most popular, although Wii Big Brain Academy is another excellent choice for getting a big brain workout.

If you do an Internet search for "seniors and Wii," you will retrieve hundreds of articles about senior centers and libraries using the Wii for recreational purposes. Even the venerable New York Public Library, in an article called "Wisdom and Wii at the Public Library," posted December 16, 2008, on NYPL.org, writes,

Exciting news for any library, anywhere with a Wii Bowling for Seniors program— you are invited to participate in the Kent Public Library Holiday Classic Wii

Bowling Tournament. Your library can enter as many four member teams as you have. Each four member team will record their best combined scores of their two best games bowled from December 15, 2008 through January 16, 2009. (Cahalan, 2008)

Academic Libraries and Wii

Even academic libraries are offering Wii activities for their student body, and at least one academic library that includes reaching out to the community as part of its mission has taken Wii to the people. In an article by Tim Gritten, Head of Library Systems at Indiana State University (ISU) in Terre Haute, Gritten describes how this academic library has embraced the Wii and is using it to engage older adults in their community. According to the article by Gritten, "Part of the Indiana State University Library's mission is to strive to engage the campus and the community. Our new logo is a comfy, red armchair; our new is motto is 'Your campus living room.' We've been able to both express the spirit of this mission and enforce our brand by taking our Wii to a local retirement center" (Gritten, 2008).

To get started, Gritten presented the concept of using the Wii with seniors to the director of leisure studies at Westminster Village, a community located a few miles from campus. The director had seen news reports of the game but was otherwise unfamiliar with it, beyond its reputation for fun. After initial contact with the director, Gritten and his staff were able to set up a program at Westminster Village. Gritten describes how "The very first Westminster resident to try the Wii saw us demonstrating tennis. She acknowledged that she had been a tennis champion 65 to 70 years earlier but that she had not played in years. It took her a few swings of the 'racket' (Wii remote) before her Mii began chasing tennis balls around the court. When she finished her short game, she admitted with a sly grin that she was sweating!" (Gritten, 2008). Numerous articles about seniors using the Wii report the same good results.

As with many Wii programs that involve seniors, Gritten states that, for obvious reasons, "Bowling has proven to be one of the most popular games" (Gritten, 2008). With the Wii, "to roll, you hold a single button on the back of the remote, then, using the exact motion you might employ with a 14-pound ball, you swing your hand and release the button at the same time that you'd release a real bowling ball. The fact that the Wii remote weighs mere ounces allows senior citizens to play a game they had long since abandoned (along with the sore shoulders and wrists). They are able to mimic the full range of possibilities that would be available at a bowling alley. You can start your throw at either side of the lane. You can throw the bowling ball at an angle. If you twist your wrist as you wave the Wii remote, your ball will curve as it slides down the lane. A single game for four inexperienced players can take 30 to 45 minutes to complete" (Gritten, 2008).

Gritten further describes how the program has grown over time. "When the ISU library staff first shared the Wii with the Westminster residents as part of a regular program, the attendance was not stellar. Part of the problem was the irregular frequency of our visits as well as the competition from other, more established events at the retirement center. Even a great program won't help anyone if it doesn't suit the target audience. So, after a few months, we changed our visits to a more convenient time for the residents and changed their frequency to weekly. We ostensibly stay for an hour, but we typically remain at Westminster for almost 2 hours to give anyone who is interested a chance to play. There are four of us, two librarians and two library staffers, involved; each one takes a turn sharing the Wii with Westminster every month" (Gritten, 2008).

The ISU staff members have regularly scheduled visits, and the program has proven to be exceedingly popular. "Frequently, a few of the more experienced residents are already waiting [when the staff members arrive]. They appreciate the opportunity to play a quick game before the program officially commences. During the regular program, residents with Alzheimer's or other forms of dementia will struggle even over the course of a few frames of bowling to remember the specific motions required. But the residents who have already played quickly support their fellow retirees" (Gritten, 2008). According to Gritten's description of the successful program,

> Even though a finite number of players can participate at any one time, the residents encourage each other, cheer at each other's successes, and blame the fickleness of the gaming system for any failures. Residents help one another learn how to play individual sports, and they show a remarkable amount of patience with their contemporaries. They have also developed individual relationships with the librarians and staff members who visit. (Gritten, 2008)

Gritten and his staff's experiences with Westminster have encouraged the library to expand on the program, and they are planning to contact other retirement centers in the community. Because the Wii allows players at one location to compete with other players at remote locations over the Internet, they plan to create tournaments for the local retirement centers to participate in.

Even though this article describes setting up a program for seniors through a university library, any type of library could follow this example and set up a similar program by partnering with senior housing or a local senior center.

HEALTH LITERACY

In a "Quick Guide to Health Literacy and Older Adults," published by the U.S. Department of Health and Human Services (2007), you can find important information regarding the issues surrounding older adults and their ability to understand health information. According to the guide, "problems with health literacy affect millions of Americans, including older adults. More than 77 million U.S. adults have basic or below basic health literacy skills. For the growing population of older Americans aged 65 years or older—expected to reach more than 71 million by 2030—difficulties with health literacy can complicate already challenging health problems (U.S. Department of Health and Human Services, 2007). While health literacy issues may not be directly related to any type of learning disability, and poor health literacy skills won't necessarily cause or contribute to a physical disability, a person's physical and mental health and the ability to understand health issues are intertwined.

What Is Health Literacy?

This guide tells us that "health literacy has to do with how well people understand and are able to use health information to take action on their health. More than just the ability to read and write, health literacy includes the ability to listen, follow directions, fill out forms, calculate using basic math, and interact with professionals and health care settings. It can also include making sense of jargon or unfamiliar cultural norms. Health literacy requires people to apply critical thinking skills to health-related matters" (U.S. Department of Health and Human Services, 2007).

According to the guide, "health literacy has been defined as 'the degree to which individuals have the capacity to obtain, process, and understand basic health information and services needed to make appropriate health decisions.' A person's health literacy is influenced by a number of factors, including basic literacy skills, the communication skills of health professionals, and the situations one encounters in the health care system. These issues affect how a person finds a doctor, reads instructions for medicine, or takes other health-related action. Also, to take such action people often need a realistic understanding of health and disease" (U.S. Department of Health and Human Services, 2007).

Health literacy includes "the ability to understand instructions on prescription drug bottles, appointment slips, medical education brochures, doctor's directions and consent forms and the ability to negotiate complex health care systems" (National Network of Libraries of Medicine, 2008). In going beyond simply the ability to read, health literacy "requires a complex group of reading, listening, analytical, and decision-making skills, and the ability to apply these skills to health situations (National Network of Libraries of Medicine, 2008). People with low health literacy skills frequently lack the knowledge and abilities necessary to handle this kind of complex analysis of the information they are receiving.

Anyone can have low health literacy, including people with good literacy skills. "In fact, most people will have trouble understanding health information at some point in their lives. For example, people experiencing serious health problems may come across specific medical terms or health information for the first time" (U.S. Department of Health and Human Services, 2007) and find that information difficult to understand.

The NAALS Report

The "Quick Guide to Health Literacy and Older Adults" uses the National Assessment of Adult Literacy (NAAL) report to document health literacy problems of older adults. "The 2003 National Assessment of Adult Literacy included the first-ever national assessment of health literacy, which found that adults age 65 and older have lower health literacy scores than all other age groups surveyed. Only 3 percent of the older adults who were surveyed were measured as proficient" (U.S. Department of Health and Human Services, 2007). As you work to improve the health of older adults in your library, you need to be aware of their health literacy needs, for several reasons:

- Health outcomes are related to health literacy. Being able to understand what is happening with your health can be a matter of life and death.
- Studies have shown that patients with low health literacy have trouble understanding health information and getting preventative health care and therefore don't get the care they need or are unable to follow medical instructions.
- Patients with low health literacy may use emergency rooms and other expensive health services more often than patients with higher health literacy skills.

The guide further states that "as many as 80 percent of older Americans have at least one chronic health condition. The more health conditions people have, the more they need to navigate the health care system and interpret complex health information. These tasks are challenging for people with low health literacy. Particular challenges for some older adults are accessing health information on the Internet and using basic math" (U.S. Department of Health and Human Services, 2007).

"Literacy problems will not always be obvious to you. Some people hide their problem out of shame, or they may not recognize the difficulty they have with reading. Such individuals may not ask important health questions, or they may misunderstand a health care provider's directions" (U.S. Department of Health and Human Services, 2007). Working with seniors as library professionals and as people who are most often in contact with older adults, it is important to be able to recognize health literacy issues with seniors and to provide programming and library collections that address these issues.

Savvy Senior Health

The National Network of Libraries of Medicine (NNLM) offers numerous training opportunities for librarians, some of which focus on seniors. NNLM works to "advance the progress of medicine and improve the public health by providing all U.S. health professionals with equal access to biomedical information and improving the public's access to information to enable them to make informed decisions about their health. The Program is coordinated by the National Library of Medicine and carried out through a nationwide network of health science libraries and information centers" (NNLM, 2006). On the training page of the NNLM Web site, at http://nnlm.gov/train ing, you can find online tutorials, fact sheets, handouts, and brochures with which you can build your own programming for older adults in your community.

The Missouri State Library, in partnership with the MidContinental Regional Medical Library, is offering a training opportunity for librarians called Savvy Senior

Health. Through this program, regional liaisons from the NNLM can schedule flexible training for library staff in libraries around the state. Contact the nearest network library to find out about health-related training opportunities for you and other librarians in your area.

PROGRAMMING IDEAS TO IMPROVE PHYSICAL AND MENTAL HEALTH IN SENIORS

In addition to gaming, electronic and otherwise, for older adults and people with disabilities, there are more traditional programs that can raise awareness about health issues and foster memory function. The Missouri State Library has an online manual filled with tips and strategies for effective library services to older adults. *Serving Seniors: A Resource Manual for Missouri Libraries* (Dahms-Stinson, 2002) has been designed to serve as a tool for all libraries to develop, plan, and expand services to Missouri citizens who are 60 and older. While the manual contains many examples of programs for older adults, here are a few more traditional programming suggestions that could benefit seniors with physical and mental impairments:

Book Discussion Groups

"Book discussion groups were one of the first activities which libraries organized and are once again popular in many communities. This group activity gives its members a chance to interact on an intellectual level and stimulates interesting conversations. With the availability of many books in large print and recorded formats it is an "inclusionary" activity. Persons with vision impairments or physical impairments can read the book in a format that best suits their needs. Book discussion groups are also library activities which can be taken to seniors where they live. Many activity directors of assisted-living facilities or senior centers are eager to find activities which encourage seniors to grow intellectually" (Dahms-Stinson, 2002).

"A successful book discussion group is one which meets the needs of the members; therefore, each book group will be structured differently. There are some overall guidelines to assure a smooth start.

- Announcement of the book discussion group should be made at least 30 days prior to the first meeting. Distribute informational flyers to bookstores, senior centers, recreation centers, doctors' offices, and places of worship.
- Encourage patrons to register for the group by calling the library. During this initial exchange patrons should be asked if they would like to have the book in another format such as large print, recorded format, or Braille. Pre-registration allows for preparation of nametags for the participants and, if requested, for reminder phone calls to be made.

- The room chosen should be relatively soundproof and free from noisy distractions to allow members to talk to each other without raising their voices. To facilitate discussion, chairs should be arranged in a circle or around a table. Members should introduce themselves, and share some information about their reading interests. The leader should face the door so that he or she may be alerted to members who arrive late.
- At the initial meeting, decide on the type of books which will be discussed, the length of the meetings, the frequency of the meetings, and whether the responsibility for leading the book discussions will remain with the library organizer or rotate among the members.
- The library organizer should choose a fairly short, positive book for the first book discussion.
- The discussion leader should have prepared at least twenty to twenty-five discussion questions prepared in the event the discussion gets bogged down. The questions should be clearly stated, using simple language.
- It is important for the leader to listen to and be sensitive to all participants. Methods might have to be devised to deal with members who dominate the discussion to allow all members to have a chance to share ideas. Conversely, quieter members may have to be prompted to discuss their thoughts" (Dahms-Stinson, 2002).

Choosing the Books

"Selecting books for a book discussion can be both fun and challenging. Books should be selected which have substance and raise questions leading to good discussions. . . . The titles chosen should not focus on topics some members of the group might find objectionable. While censorship is not advocated, avoid books that contain language or situations which may offend members of the group" (Dahms-Stinson, 2002).

Discussion Preparation

Prepare 20 to 25 questions for discussion. If preparing this number of questions is a daunting task, there are databases and Web sites that can aid in the preparation for discussion, including publisher Web sites and online book discussion clubs.

Personal Memoir Writing

An African proverb says that "'when an elder dies, a library dies as well.' Encouraging seniors to scribe their memoirs can help preserve history. Contact your local newspaper, college, or high school to enlist the help of a professional writer to lead seniors on a writing project. These memoirs can be compiled into a published document" (Dahms-Stinson, 2002). Remember that summing up is an important, natural developmental process in later life.

Memory Lane

A series of reminiscing days may be organized to allow these memories to be shared. Make use of Bi-Folkal kits or multimedia kits designed to prompt the memories of older adults and to facilitate sharing stories.

The following is a collection of programs suggested for older adults:

Program Title: Don't forget! Learning How to Remember

Program Description: The brain can be compared to a muscle, which, when exercised, can be forced to perform more efficiently, but there are limits. Thus, it helps to learn methods, tricks, and procedures to strengthen memory.

Topics

- Current learning theories and how they may be applied to increase learning and retention.
- Information on the techniques and skills for organizing thoughts, communication, learning, and remembering.
- Tricks which can be used to aid the memory processes.

Speakers

- Local mental health professional.
- Psychology professor from a local college.
- Program Title: Good Health for Seniors.
- Program Description: Growing older successfully requires the maintenance of body and mind. This series of programs will offer tips on how to take care of both the physical and psychological changes of aging.

Topics

- Lifestyle and health.
- Growing old successfully.
- Nutrition.
- Arthritis.
- Foot care.
- Other topics of interest in your surrounding community.

Speakers

- Staff of the local health department or hospital.
- Visiting Nurses Association.
- Staff of the county extension services. (Dahms-Stinson, 2002)

The *Serving Seniors* manual (Dahms-Stinson, 2002) also offers suggestions for locating Web sites and book titles that will complement each program. You can find this online manual at http://www.sos.mo.gov/library/development/services/seniors/manual.

THE NLS AND LIBRARY SERVICES TO THE BLIND AND PHYSICALLY HANDICAPPED

The National Library Services to the Blind and Physically Handicapped (NLS) offers free library service to any U.S. citizen who is unable to use standard print materials because of a visual or physical disability. This is relevant to librarians who serve older adults, as almost half the registered recipients of library service are over the age of 70. "Through a national network of cooperating libraries, NLS administers a free library program of Braille and audio materials circulated to eligible borrowers in the United States by postage-free mail" (NLS, 2009).

In *NLS at 75: National Program for Blind Readers Examines Its Past and Looks toward Its Future* (Caulton, 2006), Jane Caulton gives a history of the nation's largest library for people with disabilities, the NLS. The NLS celebrated its 75th year of service in 2006 with plans to migrate the current cassette tape service to digital format.

Senator Reed Smoot of Utah and Representative Ruth Pratt of New York sponsored the legislation for the NLS in 1931, authorizing the Library of Congress to provide embossed books for blind people in the United States and its territories. This is how the act read: Act of March 3, 1931 (Pratt-Smoot)

An Act to Provide Books for the Adult Blind

Be it enacted by the Senate and House of Representatives of the United States of America in Congress assembled, that there is hereby authorized to be appropriated annually to the Library of Congress, in addition to appropriations otherwise made to said Library, the sum of $100,000, which sum shall be expended under the direction of the Librarian of Congress to provide books for the use of the adult blind residents of the United States, including the several States, Territories, insular possessions, and the District of Columbia.

Sec. 2. The Librarian of Congress may arrange with such libraries as he may judge appropriate to serve as local or regional centers for the circulation of such books, under such conditions and regulations as he may prescribe. In the lending of such books preference shall at all times be given to the needs of blind persons who have been honorably discharged from the United States military or naval service.

Approved, March 3, 1931.
Chap. 400. Sec. 1, 46 Stat. 1487
71st Congress

The service has grown in the years since, and according to Caulton (2006), has an "appropriation in excess of $53 million and a staff of 130, NLS currently circulates more than 24 million copies of braille and recorded books and magazines by mail to approximately 500,000 readers through a network of 132 cooperating libraries." For several years, the NLS has been preparing to convert the current cassette format for the books that they distribute to digital.

"Often referred to as the library's 'talking book program,' NLS was born March 31, 1931, when President Herbert Hoover signed the Pratt-Smoot Act into law" (Caulton, 2006). According to the NLS Web site, three months after the Pratt-Smoot Act was signed into law, on July 1, 1931, the Library of Congress established Books for the Adult Blind, the division that would implement the service. The effort to improve literacy for blind people began in 1897, "when the new Congressional Library (later named the Thomas Jefferson Building) opened its doors, it provided a special reading room to share its collections with blind readers. In 1912 Congress funded the appointment of a professional librarian and the acquisition of a collection of 2,000 braille volumes" (Caulton, 2006).

Books for the Adult Blind

In 1932, "the Books for the Adult Blind program received a congressional appropriation of $100,000. That first year of operation, the staff selected 15 titles for embossing and distribution. By 1936 . . . the Library was circulating more than 6,000 braille books" (Caulton, 2006). Despite the growth in Braille book distribution, "agencies such as the American Printing House for the Blind believed that people who had lost their sight after age 50 might not have the sensitive fingers needed for learning braille. Through an amendment to the Pratt-Smoot Act in 1934, Congress appropriated $10,000 for the purchase of the first generation of talking books: books on phonograph records. However, it was not until 1947 that Congress appropriated funds for the Library to provide blind readers with the equipment on which to play the special phonograph records" (Caulton, 2006).

Books for the Blind Division

In 1943, "the Books for the Adult Blind program became the Division of Books for the Adult Blind, and the organization took over the Braille Transcribing Service from the Red Cross. With this development, the Library of Congress became responsible for the certification of all U.S. braille transcribers and proofreaders" (Caulton, 2006). In 1952, the service was expanded to include children and the word "adult" was removed from the library's title. In the 1960s, the program expanded to include music instruction materials, and in 1966, the name changed to the Division for the Blind and Physically Handicapped and included service to people with other physical impairments that prevent the reading of standard print.

"By 1978 the division had expanded from 18 regional centers to 56 regional libraries and more than 101 subregional libraries . . . [and] the organization adopted its current name, the National Library Service for the Blind and Physically Handicapped" (Caulton, 2006).

From 1969 to the present, the NLS has used analog cassettes and cassette players to distribute the recorded books, during which time NLS developed an inventory of 24 million cassettes and more than 730,000 cassette players for distribution to a growing number of patrons.

Web-Braille

"In 1999, NLS introduced Web-Braille, a Web-based service that provides users with a variety of braille books and music scores and all-braille magazines produced by NLS in an electronic form" (Caulton, 2006).

"In 1997, NLS took the next step by forming the Digital Talking-Book Standards committee, comprising more than two dozen individuals from libraries and organizations serving and representing blind and physically handicapped persons. Participants included the American Council of the Blind, the American Foundation for the Blind, the National Federation of the Blind, Recording for the Blind and Dyslexic, the University of Wisconsin's Trace Research and Development Center, and the World Blind Union" (Caulton, 2006).

"The committee worked closely with the National Information Standards Organization (NISO) to create a universal standard that would define the performance requirements for the digital talking book (DTB) and its player. In 2002 the American National Standards Institute (ANSI) approved ANSI/NISO Z39.86-2002 as the national standard for the DTB and its player. This standard, 'Specifications for the Digital Talking Book,' defined the format and content of a unified set of electronic files for the DTB and established a set of requirements for the DTB player" (Caulton, 2006).

"NLS chose the Universal Serial Bus (USB) Flash Drive for the circulation of DTBs. These credit-card-sized devices, which can hold an entire DTB, will be used with the forthcoming DTB player. The USB Flash Drive contains flash memory, a type of computer memory that can be read from, written to or erased and that does not lose its data when power is removed. This is the same kind of memory many digital cameras use to store pictures. The new medium is durable, easy to use, reusable and recyclable" (Caulton, 2006).

In 2009 NLS will begin to replace its existing cassette-based talking book system with the new DTBs. This has distinct advantages of digital over the analog technology, such as flash memory cartridges that

- Are portable and easier to use.
- Have larger storage densities and capacities.
- Provide better audio quality.
- Have a simple duplication process.
- Allow cartridges to be reused while retaining high-quality audio reproduction.

Another advantage is the digital players that

- Are portable and easier to use.
- Are more robust and resistant to damage.

- Are smaller, more compact, and lighter weight.
- Have no moving parts, consume less power, and have longer battery operation.
- Are more reliable and have fewer malfunctions with simpler repairs. (Smith, 2009)

The digital transition will continue to provide the same high-quality narration NLS patrons have come to expect.

ELIGIBILITY OF BLIND AND OTHER PHYSICALLY HANDICAPPED PERSONS FOR LOAN OF LIBRARY MATERIALS

According to the NLS Web site, there are specific eligibility requirements that patrons must meet in order to receive the books by mail at no cost.

The following persons are eligible for service:

A. Blind persons whose visual acuity, as determined by competent authority, is 20/200 or less in the better eye with correcting lenses, or whose widest diameter of visual field subtends an angular distance no greater than 20 degrees.
B. Other physically handicapped persons are eligible as follows:

1. Persons whose visual disability, with correction and regardless of optical measurement, is certified by competent authority as preventing the reading of standard printed material
2. Persons certified by competent authority as unable to read or unable to use standard printed material as a result of physical limitations.
3. Persons certified by competent authority as having a reading disability resulting from organic dysfunction and of sufficient severity to prevent their reading printed material in a normal manner.

Certifying Authority

In cases of blindness, visual impairment, or physical limitations, "competent authority" is defined to include doctors of medicine; doctors of osteopathy; ophthalmologists; optometrists; registered nurses; therapists; and professional staff of hospitals, institutions, and public or private welfare agencies (e.g., social workers, case workers, counselors, rehabilitation teachers, and superintendents). In the absence of any of these, certification may be made by professional librarians or by any person whose competence under specific circumstances is acceptable to the Library of Congress.

In the case of reading disability from organic dysfunction, competent authority is defined as doctors of medicine and doctors of osteopathy who may consult with colleagues in associated disciplines.

Residency or U.S. Citizenship

Eligible readers must be residents of the United States, including the several states, territories, insular possessions, and the District of Columbia; or, American citizens domiciled abroad.

Lending of Materials and Classes of Borrowers

Veterans

In the lending of books, recordings, playback equipment, musical scores, instructional texts, and other specialized materials, preference shall be given at all times to the needs of the blind and other physically handicapped persons who have been honorably discharged from the armed forces of the United States.

Institutions

The reading materials and playback equipment for the use of blind and physically handicapped persons may be loaned to individuals who qualify, to institutions such as nursing homes and hospitals, and to schools for the blind or physically handicapped for the use by such persons only. The reading materials and playback equipment may also be used in public or private schools where handicapped students are enrolled; however, the students in public or private schools must be certified as eligible on an individual basis and must be the direct and only recipients of the materials and equipment. (NLS, 2006)

The 10^2 Talking-Book Club (Ten Squared Club)

In addition to recorded books by mail, the NLS offers foreign language materials, a music collection (including music scores in Braille), a children's program, and something called the 10^2 Talking-Book Club. The 10^2 (ten squared) Talking-Book Club honors centenarians who are users of talking books through membership in the club. According to Frank Kurt Cylke, the director of NLS,

> The 10^2 Talking-Book Club was conceived to recognize the accomplishments of the national reading program's centenarians. Through induction ceremonies in all states . . . the Library of Congress will honor these . . . individuals. The events will highlight the reading services provided by each state and also increase the awareness of others eligible to join their free local or state reading program. (NLS, 2004)

Ceremonies to honor these centenarians were held in several states in 2005 and 2006, including the Wolfner Library in Missouri. "Missouri's Wolfner Library for the Blind and Physically Handicapped inducted 10 talking-book readers into the 10^2 Talking-Book Club at the St. Louis Public Library on September 22, 2005. "One-hundred-and-three-year-old Katharine Chambers of St. Louis, who is Missouri's first 10^2 inductee, was guest of honor. Missouri secretary of state Robin Carnahan and NLS Network Division chief Carolyn Hoover Sung presented Chambers with a certificate, a pin, and a letter from NLS director Frank Kurt Cylke" (NLS, 2005).

Braille and Audio Reading Download (BARD)

The NLS developed an accessible Web site as a pilot project for downloading DTBs in February of 2006. The download pilot was expanded in the fall of 2007 and is expected to be a full-scale service in 2009. The current site has over 14,000 titles available for download.

A patron wishing to participate in the Braille and Audio Reading Download (BARD) should:

- Be an active patron of a cooperating network library
- Have access to a player capable of playing NLS-produced digital talking books
- Have high-speed Internet service such as DSL or cable
- Have access to a computer connected to the Internet for downloading and un-zipping books and/or magazines
- Have access to an active e-mail address (NLS, 2007)

Patrons can download books onto a NLS flash cartridge or a standard USB drive—the new digital machine read both storage devices, with a limitation of one book per device. Fortunately, these devices can be used again numerous times. There are third-party vendor machines that meet NLS security requirements to play NLS digital books that allow more than on book to be downloaded to a storage device. In addition, many patrons will save books on their computer hard drives for future use, in effect creating their own personal library of talking books.

The availability of electronic delivery of talking books and magazines is creating a paradigm shift in reading habits of patrons of NLS library services. Removing the dependence on the U.S. Postal Service for book delivery and eliminating restrictive library loan requirements allows for 24/7 access of books and magazines and ownership of reading materials, and many users of the BARD system are extremely happy with the outcome.

Free Recorded Literature Online

LibriVox was started in August 2005, by Hugh McGuire, a Montreal-based writer and Web developer. The written objective of LibriVox, as found on their Web site, is: "To make all books in the public domain available, for free, in audio format on the internet" (LibriVox, n.d.). The fundamental principles of LibriVox include the following:

- Librivox is a non-commercial, non-profit, and ad-free project
- Librivox donates its recordings to the public domain
- Librivox is powered by volunteers
- Librivox maintains a loose and open structure
- Librivox welcomes all volunteers from across the globe, in all languages (LibriVox, n.d.)

The LibriVox Web site offers the following explanation of their program:

> LibriVox volunteers record chapters of books in the public domain, and then we release the audio files back onto the net for free. All our audio is in the public domain, so you may use it for whatever purpose you wish.
>
> Volunteering for LibriVox is easy and does not require any experience with recording or audio engineering or acting or public speaking. All you need is a computer, some free recording software, and your own voice. We accept all volunteers in all languages, with all kinds of accents. You don't need to audition or send us samples. We'll accept you no matter what you sound like.
>
> We operate almost exclusively through Internet communications on our forum, where all your questions will be answered by our friendly community. We have a flat structure, designed to let people do just what they want to do. (LibriVox, n.d.)

On the links page of LibriVox, you will find links to numerous other recording projects, including podcasts, blogs, and other audio literature projects. Visit the LibriVox Web site at http://librivox.org/.

CONCLUSION

While not exactly a specialized field, serving seniors does require some additional knowledge. Changes to eyesight, hearing, brain function, and other physical changes make serving older adults in libraries a challenge, but the rewards are many. By paying careful attention to the special needs of older adults and youthful Baby Boomers, you can create successful programs within your library that will enhance their quality of life and ensure that learning is indeed a lifelong process. With your help, older adults in your community can say along with Maurice Chevalier's character in the movie version of the musical *Gigi*, "I'm so glad I'm not young anymore!"

CHAPTER 5

Library Services to Persons with Mental and Learning Disabilities

Working with the public in a library setting, staff members are likely to encounter any or all of the mental disabilities discussed in this chapter. Since few of us have had extensive education in causes of or treatment for persons with mental disabilities, this chapter offers a brief introduction to help you begin to understand the illnesses. Should you have a regular patron with any of these illnesses, you should seek additional help in handling the situation. The chapter further covers library services to the homeless who may or may not have mental disabilities.

In "Changing Our Minds: Those with Mental Illness Need Understanding and Respect" (Whitbeck, 2008), Faye Whitbeck addresses the suffering that people with mental disorders face because of social stigma and stereotyping. She suggests that it is easier to empathize with people with mental illness when reading about their challenges and suffering than it is when actually dealing with someone with mental illness, and librarians increasingly are faced with the challenge of dealing with those with mental illness, sometimes without the empathy we would like to see exhibited by our fellow professionals.

On the blog @ the Library, you will find a frank discussion of what it's like to deal with the mentally ill and homeless on a regular basis at http://librarianwoes.wordpress.com.

In the entry "Parade of Freaks" (http://librarianwoes.wordpress.com/2008/01/02/ parade-of-freaks), one less than happy library worker describes one day of dealing with patrons, some of whom have legitimate mental illness or disabilities and probably just a few neighborhood characters:

> Today was like the dam burst, or like the Freak Bus let off right in front of our door. After two weeks of mellowness we had an exceptionally busy day that included appearances by numerous people requesting income tax forms (they must be expecting windfall returns), The Hobo, Special Ed, who kept orbiting the Reference Desk making intermittent appearances, our neighborhood transvestite who breezed in and breezed out after browsing Children's Videos, and Porn Man who, pack in tow, dropped anchor for the duration of the evening. I'm actually surprised that we weren't inundated by the homeless since it's supposed to hit a balmy 13° outside tonight.
>
> Anyway, Porn Man stuck to his M.O. by unpacking his mammoth backpack near the Internet workstations where he meticulous [sic] laid out in linear fashion, two pink razors, a pink can of Skintimate shaving cream, a bottle of orange Gatorade, and a jar of Tums . . . LMAO!! He then plugged both his video camera, and cell phone into the wall behind our microfilm cabinets allowing them to charge. He used up his time, presumably scouring the Internet for new material to spank off to, and saving only the "best" stuff onto his flash drive for later perusal.
>
> True to form, after his time was up on the Internet, he asked to sign in to one of our word processing machines, presumably to leisurely view what he just downloaded. After a while, he began printing, but much to his dismay, the ink was running low so he summoned me over to fetch a new cartridge. I obliged. Just before closing, he came over to the Desk, handed me . . . [an] image . . . and said that it was still printing "like this." ("Parade of Freaks," 2008)

It undoubtedly makes us sad for our fellow professionals to read these stories. We feel badly for our colleagues who have gone to college and worked to obtain an advanced degree, only to find themselves dealing with patrons like "Special Ed" and "Porn Man," whose information needs might not fall into the norm. In a society that casually uses words like "crazy," "psycho," "retard," or "wacko" to characterize the mentally ill person or even each other in jest, even those who consider themselves to be intellectually enlightened sometimes find themselves using these terms insensitively, as illustrated by "Parade of Freaks." While we can all empathize with the librarians and their plight, we should consider saving some of that empathy for our patrons with mental illness. Seemingly harmless words resonate with those already struggling to function in society, and as Whitbeck (2008) suggests, "just hearing them can make the difference between moving forward with hope; or hiding alone in pain."

According to Whitbeck (2008), "diseases of the mind are viewed differently from other diseases largely because of the organ in which they occur. Even the label 'mental illness,' sets them apart from diabetes, arthritis, heart disease, cancer and other illnesses. Because a mental disease is in the brain itself, the perception is that one is 'choosing' to be ill," which might also lead to the conclusion that it is okay to disdain those with mental illness. If it's all in your head, why can't you just change your mind? we might ask. Even common expressions that we use every day, such as, "Oh, I changed my mind," ingrain in those of us without any form of mental illness that we should have complete control over our minds. Even some psychotherapy treatments, like cognitive therapy, suggest that if you have a sad thought you can replace it with a happy one, until, through repetition, you learn new patterns of thinking. Cognitive therapy can work with some forms of depression and behavioral problems, but there are mental illnesses that require medical treatment. And, as with any disease, when it "is acknowledged and treated, [it] has a great impact on the health of the sufferer" (Whitbeck, 2008).

MENTAL ILLNESS AND HOMELESSNESS

It is a well-known fact that in many major metropolitan areas, dealing with the homeless, many of whom are mentally ill, is an increasing problem in libraries. Just ask the woeful librarian of @ the Library.

According to the Substance Abuse and Mental Health Services Administration (2003), "thirty-nine percent [of homeless people] report some form of mental health problem, and 20–25 percent meet criteria for serious mental illness." In comparison, "an estimated 26.2 percent of Americans ages 18 and older—about one in four adults—suffer from a diagnosable mental disorder . . . [and] only about 6 percent, or 1 in 17 . . . suffer from a serious mental illness" (National Institute of Mental Health, 2008). In a 2008 survey performed by the U.S. Conference of Mayors, of the "23 cities that provided this information reported that 26 percent of their homeless population suffered from a serious mental illness" (U.S. Conference of Mayors, 2008).

Deinstitutionalization

"The growth in homelessness is not attributable to the release of seriously mentally ill people from institutions. Most patients were released from mental hospitals in the 1950s and 1960s, yet vast increases in homelessness did not occur until the 1980s, when incomes and housing options for those living on the margins began to diminish rapidly" (National Coalition for the Homeless, 2005). "Over 40 years have passed since many psychiatric institutions in the United States were closed . . . but the promise of community-based, outpatient mental health services has not been kept—particularly for many of the sickest and poorest of the mentally ill whose only refuge is the streets" (Health Care for the Homeless Clinicians' Network, 2000). This has resulted in the problems that we have today. "A new wave of deinstitutionalization and the denial of services or premature and unplanned discharge brought about by managed care arrangements may be also be contributing to the continued presence of seriously mentally ill persons within the homeless population" (National Coalition for the Homeless, 2005).

"Mental disorders prevent people from carrying out essential aspects of daily life, such as self-care, household management and interpersonal relationships. Homeless people with mental disorders remain homeless for longer periods of time and have less contact with family and friends" (National Coalition for the Homeless, 2005). "[P]ersons with serious mental illness may not understand that they are ill and need care. Severe and persistent mental illnesses (SPMI)—including schizophrenia, bipolar disorder, major depression and dementia—impair judgement, conceptual understanding and the capacity to make appropriate behavior decisions. People with these disorders typically misinterpret what others say and react with irrational fear or anger, often alienating friends, family and caregivers" (Health Care for the Homeless Clinicians' Network, 2000).

Mentally ill homeless people "encounter more barriers to employment, tend to be in poorer physical health, and have more contact with the legal system than homeless people who do not suffer from mental disorder. All people with mental disorders, including those who are homeless, require ongoing access to a full range of treatment and rehabilitation services to lessen the impairment and disruption produced by their condition. However, most people with mental disorder do not need hospitalization, and even fewer require long-term institutional care" (National Coalition for the Homeless, 2005).

LIBRARY SERVICES TO THE HOMELESS

Public libraries in major metropolitan areas, mid-sized cities, and probably even small towns have been a daytime sanctuary for the homeless, or those who live in group homes. Housed in shelters or group homes at night, many of the homeless are left to their own devices during the day time, and libraries are increasingly offering services targeted to the homeless population. Even in a mid-sized parish library in rural Louisiana, there were a couple of citizens who slept their day away at the computers each day.

In "When the Rights of the Many Outweigh the Rights of the Few: The 'Legitimate' Versus the Homeless Patron in the Public Library," Julie Murphy (1999) present arguments in favor of library access for the homeless. Murphy writes,

> Not only do homeless people have the same rights as others, but it is illegal to treat them differently, and libraries that do so may be vulnerable to lawsuits. Furthermore, the library can provide a place for the mentally ill to interact with normal society. The library can also provide an important community service by identifying and connecting homeless people with the proper social service agencies, even working actively with those agencies to create safe spaces for the homeless to occupy. Since many homeless people are also mentally ill, and mental illness is equivalent to a physical illness or disability, it could be argued that homeless people need to be accorded rights under the Americans with Disabilities

Act (ADA). This point is often overlooked when dealing with mentally ill people, due to our society's tendency to discount the validity of mental illness as a medical problem. (Murphy, 1999)

At the very least, you and your library staff should be educated about the issues homeless people face and trained to deal with homeless people. Creating policies that are administered fairly can help patrons and staff to understand appropriate library behavior. Librarians should also provide collection development in information areas important to the homeless, as well as helping to educate the public about their conditions and lives. Some libraries are doing much more than that.

In an article in *USA Today* (Motsinger, 2007), Motsinger describes some ways in which libraries serve the homeless and are making a concerted effort to do so. These services vary and the examples are from large public libraries, but they can be applied to your library when the situations are the same, such as the example below of bringing homeless children to your library for story time. Here are those examples:

- In Washington, D.C., the Martin Luther King Jr. Memorial Library has begun seminars about library resources and health care services for the homeless. The library plans to offer music appreciation and arts classes to homeless patrons.
- Jacksonville Public Library teaches Internet use to homeless job-seekers.
- The Free Library of Philadelphia pays homeless people to work as bathroom attendants at the central library.
- The San Francisco Public Library has two part-time staffers who refer the homeless to housing and mental health agencies.
- The Los Angeles Public Library has a five-day summer camp for homeless children. In July, a magician, mime, musician and storyteller will perform and teach.
- Volunteers take children from homeless shelters to New York Public Library branches for monthly story time sessions. (Motsinger, 2007)

Although some librarians find helping those who need the most help a rewarding experience, others are not so enthusiastic about the prospect, as is evidenced in the tone of the woeful librarian in the @ the Library blog. According to Motsinger, library visitors often complain about people "panhandling, staring or saying inappropriate things to children" (Motsinger, 2007). These are real issues, and many librarians have responded by implementing policies to deter all sorts of behavior, including a no sleeping policy.

LIBRARY POLICIES THAT AFFECT THE HOMELESS

In another era, sleeping in the public library might have historically been the privilege of the pink-cheeked older middle-class gentleman who just happened to nod off over the newspaper after lunch. With the influx of homeless and mentally ill after deinstitutionalization, sleeping in the library has become a problem. It's still sleeping, it's still the same activity, but maybe it's just a different class of people who are doing the sleeping? We can't help but wonder if the libraries that have no sleeping policies gently awaken the older pillar of the community who does happen to nod off for a moment, or is the policy discriminatory?

Sleeping and Other Problem Behavior Policies

Since library boards and administrators have felt the need to create and enforce policies regarding disruptive behaviors, including sleeping, in their libraries, it might be a good idea to take a look at a few of those policies, for the purpose of determining if your own policies are too stringent or not stringent enough. Four policies from libraries ranging from large metropolitan to smaller county libraries are provided for you. One of these excerpts from behavior policies relating to the types of behavior that the homeless or mentally ill might be taking into the library is shown in the following box text. Three others are found in Appendix B.

Randolph County Public Library Disruptive Behavior Policy

The objective of this policy is to ensure that the Randolph County Public Library provides for each user a welcoming, pleasant and safe environment, conducive to reading, studying, seeking information, meeting friends and collaborating; and free from harassment, physical discomfort, danger and psychological and emotional stress. In the pursuit of this objective, the library board shall consider the following to be disruptive and unacceptable behavior in the public service areas of the library:

- Sustained loud conversation, or noise, that rises above the ambient noise in the library;
- Obscene or abusive language or gestures;
- Threats, abuse or physical harm to library patrons or staff;
- Blocking or in any way interfering with the free movement of any person;
- Following a person around the building or grounds, or other harassing behavior, such as staring, or other intimidating acts;
- Engaging in disorderly conduct, committing a nuisance or unreasonably disturbing and offending library users;
- Carrying weapons of any sort;
- Smoking, or the use of any tobacco product;
- Consumption or exchange of alcoholic beverages;
- Consumption of food, and consumption of uncovered beverages, except in designated areas;
- Soliciting or selling of any kind, except for library-related fundraising events;
- Taking of surveys without approval;
- Sleeping in the library;
- Distribution of leaflets, or posting notices without authorization;

- Destruction of, or damage to, or theft of library property from building or grounds;
- Removal of material from the library collection without authorization through established lending procedure;
- Bringing animals, other than service animals, into the building;
- Use of library telephones by any person other than library personnel, unless approved;
- Entry into non-public areas except by invitation or approval of library personnel;
- Failure to leave the library promptly at closing;
- Failure to respond to requests from library staff members in regard to this policy;
- Disruptive behavior on library property may result in exclusion from the library and/or arrest.

Randolph County (North Carolina) Public Library Disruptive Behavior Policy

Adopted July 16, 1998 by the Randolph Public Library, Revised August 2004.

Sanford Berman, founder of the American Library Association's Hunger, Homelessness and Poverty Task Force, is quoted in the Motsinger (2007) *USA Today* article, stating: "others complain about patrons' grooming. Libraries . . . have hygiene rules. [These rules] must be administered evenly. 'That kind of rule should be equally applied to a suburban matron doused in perfume,' he says." We would add that other policies, such as those regarding sleeping in the library, should be administered fairly, as well.

Dealing with the homeless and mentally disabled patron is, without a doubt, one of the greatest challenges that library professionals face today. It is important to make informed policy decisions regarding this troubled and troubling portion of the population.

SERVICES TO PERSONS WITH DEMENTIA

In *A Challenge for Public Libraries: Guidelines for Library Services to Persons with Dementia* (Mortensen & Nielsen, 2007), Helle Arendrup Mortensen and Gyda Skat Nielsen offer suggestions for library staff involved in serving person with dementia. While working with people with dementia in the library might not be a tremendous issue, those who serve in-home library patrons or who do outreach to skilled nursing centers or nursing homes will likely come in contact with more patrons with some form of dementia.

According to this report, currently there are an estimated 24 million people worldwide with some form of dementia, and this figure is set to increase to more than 81 million people by 2040. While librarians might not immediately come to mind when thinking of the types of professionals caring for persons with dementia, most public libraries provide services to meet the informational and recreational needs of all population groups, and with the increase in the number of those over age 65, and the decline of funding for services to older adults, it is most likely that you or staff members in your library will provide services to people suffering from dementia.

Mortensen and Nielsen provide the following general suggestions for communicating with those with dementia:

- Make eye contact so the person knows you are talking *to* and not *about* him/her
- Make sure to get the person's attention before speaking
- Speak clearly and slowly. Make eye contact
- Pay attention to the body language of the person with dementia as well as your own, since non-verbal communication is very important for persons with language impairments
- Use simple language, short sentences, and avoid foreign words
- Use repetitions and consistent phrasing to avoid confusion
- Be a creative listener and show understanding, tolerance, and respect
- Give the person with dementia enough time to answer and ask questions that can be answered with a simple "yes" or "no." Avoid open-ended questions.
- Include everyday topics in your conversation, e.g., the weather, and references to familiar objects that may trigger the memory
- Be calm and supportive and use comforting gestures (Mortensen & Nielsen, 2007, p. 8)

Tailoring library services and specific materials can have positive effects on persons with dementia, and these suggestions can be useful for those choosing library materials for patrons or planning programming. It is important to know that people with dementia might react or behave differently, and prior to visiting with dementia patients, "library staff [should] consult with professionals in the field . . . and, if possible, spend some time with a mentor observing dementia patients in a care facility" (Mortensen & Nielsen, 2007, p. 10). It will make the first visit with the patron/patient a more pleasant and rewarding experience.

Library Materials for Persons with Dementia

Mortensen and Nielsen suggest that

Books and audiovisual materials can contribute to the quality of institutional life. By evoking pleasant memories you help the patrons regain their feeling of identity. These persons may have had specific hobbies and interests during their lifetime. Books and music may remind the patrons of these interests and stir memories of childhood, youth, working life and family. (Mortensen & Nielsen, 2007, p. 11)

Further, these authors recommend the following types of materials:

- Illustrated books
  "Persons with dementia usually like books with big and clear illustrations, particularly photos. Popular subjects are animals, flowers, fashion, children, countries, old cars, etc." (Mortensen & Nielsen, 2007, p. 11). Find out what

the person is interested in. Even those with dementia will spark at the sight of a favorite item. "Children's picture books with big and clear illustrations are appropriate" (Mortensen & Nielsen, 2007, p. 11).

- Books for reading aloud
Read aloud, particularly books that are "short and have a simple story line" (Mortensen & Nielsen, 2007, p. 11). Low literacy books and graphic novels "are also appropriate as they are written in short sentences and have an uncomplicated plot. Essays, fairytales and short stories are recommended. Books with jokes, rhymes and jingles from old times and very easy quizzes have proven popular. Some persons with dementia enjoy listening to familiar poems and songs. They often join the singing and show an amazing ability in remembering the text" (Mortensen & Nielsen, 2007, p. 11), as songs and rhymes that were ingrained into the memory in childhood remain in accessible neural paths in the brain.

- Thematic books
Choose books "in connection with holiday celebrations, e.g. Christmas and Easter, theme books may be used as conversation starters about old traditions, holiday meals, decorations, etc." (Mortensen & Nielsen, 2007, p. 11).

- "Local history is popular and . . . books about the past are very suitable for reminiscing and for conversation groups" (Mortensen & Nielsen, 2007, p. 11).
- Music
Mortensen and Nielsen suggest that "music is an important medium in the interaction with persons with dementia. Verbal communication is often difficult, but singing, dancing and listening to music are good alternatives" (Mortensen & Nielsen, 2007, p. 11), as musical tunes and lyrics can be easily ingrained in memory through repetition. "Music gives persons with dementia an opportunity to express feelings, interact with other persons, remember the past, express his/her personality, [and] reduce anxiety and restlessness. Music can be used in small groups or with individuals. The music should be popular and familiar. Examples [include] calm classical music, e.g., special editions created for persons with dementia; music and songs with a special theme, e.g., the seasons, flowers, love or loss; meditative music for relaxation; and video and DVDs. Everybody likes to watch a good movie. Persons with dementia enjoy watching old movies in their native language and from their own country. These movies bring back memories from 'the good old days.' Films about local history and nature are also popular" (Mortensen & Nielsen, 2007, p. 11).

- Reminiscence Kits or Bi-Folkal kits
"Reminiscence kits are very helpful in stimulating memories. . . . [T]he kits are theme defined and may contain old cooking utensils, old toilet articles for ladies or gentlemen, school books and supplies, craft items and tools,

gardening items, etc." (Mortensen & Nielsen, 2007, p. 12). Many libraries create their own reminiscence kits, but a large selection of kits is also available for purchase from http://www.bifolkal.org. According to the Web site, with Bi-Folkal kits, "*Remembering* is the first word of every kit title, and it's the first focus of every item we produce. Reminiscence programs can meet many needs: the need of the family to know and embrace its history; the need of older adults to put their lives in perspective; and the need of the community to understand and honor the accomplishments of earlier generations" (Bi-Folkal Productions, n.d.).

- Materials on dementia for staff and caregivers
  Finally, don't forget to include "a selection of books and other information materials about dementia [for] library staff and patient care givers. It is recommended that public libraries offer a broad selection of books and other materials on dementia as part of their general collection" (Mortensen & Nielsen, 2007, p. 12).

MENTAL DISORDERS YOU MIGHT OR MIGHT NOT RECOGNIZE

The National Institute of Mental Health (NIMH) offers information on a variety of mental disorders, the symptoms of some of which you may or may not recognize from your work with the general public. NIMH envisions a world in which mental illnesses are prevented and cured, and its mission is to "transform the understanding and treatment of mental illnesses through basic and clinical research, paving the way for prevention, recovery and cure" (NIMH, 2009). The NIMH Web site offers "Mental Health Topics" at http://www.nimh.nih.gov/health/topics, some of which we reference here, in an effort to foster understanding of library patrons with mental illness. According to "Mental Health Topics":

Panic Disorder

Panic disorder is a real illness that can be successfully treated. It is characterized by sudden attacks of terror, usually accompanied by a pounding heart, sweatiness, weakness, faintness, or dizziness. During these attacks, people with panic disorder may flush or feel chilled; their hands may tingle or feel numb; and they may experience nausea, chest pain, or smothering sensations. Panic attacks usually produce a sense of unreality, a fear of impending doom, or a fear of losing control.

A fear of one's own unexplained physical symptoms is also a symptom of panic disorder. People having panic attacks sometimes believe they are having heart attacks, losing their minds, or on the verge of death. They can't predict when or where an attack will occur, and between episodes many worry intensely and dread the next attack.

Panic attacks can occur at any time, even during sleep. An attack usually peaks within 10 minutes, but some symptoms may last much longer.

Panic disorder affects about 6 million American adults and is twice as common in women as men. Panic attacks often begin in late adolescence or early adulthood, but not everyone who experiences panic attacks will develop panic disorder. Many people have just one attack and never have another. The tendency to develop panic attacks appears to be inherited.

People who have full-blown, repeated panic attacks can become very disabled by their condition and should seek treatment before they start to avoid places or situations where panic attacks have occurred. For example, if a panic attack happened in an elevator, someone with panic disorder may develop a fear of elevators that could affect the choice of a job or an apartment, and restrict where that person can seek medical attention or enjoy entertainment.

Some people's lives become so restricted that they avoid normal activities, such as grocery shopping or driving. About one-third become housebound or may confront a feared situation only when accompanied by a spouse or other trusted person. When the condition progresses this far, it is called agoraphobia, or fear of open spaces. [Agoraphobics might end up requesting in-home library service from your library.]

Early treatment can often prevent agoraphobia, but people with panic disorder may sometimes go from doctor to doctor for years and visit the emergency room repeatedly before someone correctly diagnoses their condition. This is unfortunate, because panic disorder is one of the most treatable of all the anxiety disorders, responding in most cases to certain kinds of medication or certain kinds of cognitive psychotherapy, which help change thinking patterns that lead to fear and anxiety.

Panic disorder is often accompanied by other serious problems, such as depression, drug abuse, or alcoholism. (NIMH, n.d.)

Obsessive-Compulsive Disorder, OCD

People with obsessive-compulsive disorder (OCD) have persistent, upsetting thoughts (obsessions) and use rituals (compulsions) to control the anxiety these thoughts produce. Most of the time, the rituals end up controlling them.

For example, if people are obsessed with germs or dirt, they may develop a compulsion to wash their hands over and over again. If they develop an obsession with intruders, they may lock and relock their doors many times before going to bed. Being afraid of social embarrassment may prompt people with OCD to comb their hair compulsively in front of a mirror—sometimes they get "caught" in the mirror and can't move away from it. Performing such rituals is not pleasurable. At best, it produces temporary relief from the anxiety created by obsessive thoughts.

Other common rituals include a need to repeatedly check things, touch things (especially in a particular sequence), or count things. Some common obsessions include having frequent thoughts of violence and harming loved ones, persistently thinking about performing sexual acts the person dislikes, or having thoughts that are prohibited by religious beliefs. People with OCD may also be preoccupied with order and symmetry, have difficulty throwing things out (so they accumulate), or hoard unneeded items.

[Depending on the severity of the compulsion, people with OCD can end up being reclusive and could be among those that apply for in-home library service.]

OCD affects about 2.2 million American adults, and the problem can be accompanied by eating disorders, other anxiety disorders, or depression. It strikes men and women in roughly equal numbers and usually appears in childhood, adolescence, or early adulthood. One-third of adults with OCD develop symptoms as children, and research indicates that OCD might run in families. (NIMH, n.d.)

Bipolar Disorder

Bipolar disorder causes dramatic mood swings—from overly "high" and/or irritable to sad and hopeless, and then back again, often with periods of normal mood in between. Severe changes in energy and behavior go along with these changes in mood. The periods of highs and lows are called episodes of mania and depression.

Signs and symptoms of mania (or a manic episode) include:

- Increased energy, activity, and restlessness
- Excessively "high," overly good, euphoric mood
- Extreme irritability
- Racing thoughts and talking very fast, jumping from one idea to another
- Distractibility, can't concentrate well
- Little sleep needed
- Unrealistic beliefs in one's abilities and powers
- Poor judgment
- Spending sprees
- A lasting period of behavior that is different from usual
- Increased sexual drive
- Abuse of drugs, particularly cocaine, alcohol, and sleeping medications
- Provocative, intrusive, or aggressive behavior
- Denial that anything is wrong

A manic episode is diagnosed if elevated mood occurs with 3 or more of the other symptoms most of the day, nearly every day, for 1 week or longer. If the mood is irritable, 4 additional symptoms must be present.

Signs and symptoms of depression (or a depressive episode) include:

- Lasting sad, anxious, or empty mood
- Feelings of hopelessness or pessimism
- Feelings of guilt, worthlessness, or helplessness
- Loss of interest or pleasure in activities once enjoyed, including sex
- Decreased energy, a feeling of fatigue or of being "slowed down."
- Difficulty concentrating, remembering, making decisions
- Restlessness or irritability
- Sleeping too much, or can't sleep
- Change in appetite and/or unintended weight loss or gain
- Chronic pain or other persistent bodily symptoms that are not caused by physical illness or injury
- Thoughts of death or suicide, or suicide attempts

A depressive episode is diagnosed if 5 or more of these symptoms last most of the day, nearly every day, for a period of 2 weeks or longer.

A mild to moderate level of mania is called hypomania. Hypomania may feel good to the person who experiences it and may even be associated with good functioning and enhanced productivity. Thus even when family and friends learn to recognize the mood swings as possible bipolar disorder, the person may deny that anything is wrong. Without proper treatment, however, hypomania can become severe mania in some people or can switch into depression.

Sometimes, severe episodes of mania or depression include symptoms of psychosis or psychotic symptoms. Common psychotic symptoms are hallucinations (hearing, seeing, or otherwise sensing the presence of things not actually there) and delusions (false, strongly held beliefs not influenced by logical reasoning or explained by a person's usual cultural concepts). Psychotic symptoms in bipolar disorder tend to reflect the extreme mood state at the time. For example, delusions of grandiosity, such as believing one is the President or has special powers or wealth, may occur during mania; delusions of guilt or worthlessness, such as believing that one is ruined and penniless or has committed some terrible crime, may appear during depression. People with bipolar disorder who have these symptoms are sometimes incorrectly diagnosed as having schizophrenia, another severe mental illness.

It may be helpful to think of the various mood states in bipolar disorder as a spectrum or continuous range. At one end is severe depression, above which is moderate depression and then mild low mood, which many people call "the blues" when it is short-lived but is termed "dysthymia" when it is chronic. Then there is normal or balanced mood, above which comes hypomania (mild to moderate mania), and then severe mania. (NIMH, n.d.)

Schizophrenia

The symptoms of schizophrenia fall into three broad categories:

- Positive symptoms affect both thoughts and perceptions and they include hallucinations, delusions, and disordered thinking.
- Negative symptoms represent a loss or a decrease in the ability to initiate plans, speak, express emotion, or find pleasure in everyday life. These symptoms are harder to recognize as part of the disorder and can be mistaken for laziness or depression.
- Cognitive symptoms (or cognitive deficits) are problems with attention, certain types of memory, and the executive functions that allow us to plan and organize. Cognitive deficits can also be difficult to recognize as part of the disorder but are the most disabling because of their impact on one's day-to-day life functioning.

Positive symptoms

Positive symptoms are psychotic behaviors not seen in healthy people. People with positive symptoms often "lose touch" with reality. These symptoms can come and go. Sometimes they are severe and at other times hardly noticeable, depending on whether the individual is receiving treatment. They include the following:

Hallucinations are things a person sees, hears, smells, or feels that no one else can see, hear, smell, or feel. "Voices" are the most common type of hallucination in schizophrenia. Many people with the disorder hear voices. The voices may talk to the person about his or her behavior, order the person to do things, or warn the person of danger. Sometimes the voices talk to each other. People with schizophrenia may hear these voices for a long time before family and friends notice the problem.

Other types of hallucinations include seeing people or objects that are not there, smelling odors that no one else detects, and feeling things like invisible fingers touching their bodies when no one is near.

Delusions are false beliefs that are not part of the person's culture and do not change. The person believes delusions even after other people prove that the beliefs are not true or logical. People with schizophrenia can have delusions that are quite bizarre, such as believing that neighbors can control their behavior with magnetic waves. They may also believe that people on television are directing special messages to them, or that radio stations are broadcasting their thoughts aloud to others. Sometimes they believe they are someone else, such as a famous historical figure. They may have paranoid delusions and believe that others are trying to harm them, such as by cheating, harassing, poisoning, spying on, or plotting against them or the people they care about. These beliefs are called "delusions of persecution."

Thought disorders are unusual or dysfunctional ways of thinking. One form of thought disorder is called "disorganized thinking." This is when a person has trouble organizing his or her thoughts or connecting them logically. They may speak in a garbled way that is hard to understand. Another form is called "thought blocking." This is when a person stops speaking abruptly in the middle of a thought. When asked why he or she stopped talking, the person may say that it felt as if the thought had been taken out of his or her head. Finally, a person with a thought disorder might make up meaningless words, or "neologisms."

Movement disorders may appear as agitated body movements. A person with a movement disorder may repeat certain motions over and over. In the other extreme, a person may become catatonic. Catatonia is a state in which a person does not move and does not respond to others. Catatonia is rare today, but it was more common when treatment for schizophrenia was not available.

Negative symptoms

Negative symptoms are associated with disruptions to normal emotions and behaviors. These symptoms are harder to recognize as part of the disorder and can be mistaken for depression or other conditions. These symptoms include the following:

- "Flat affect" (a person's face does not move or he or she talks in a dull or monotonous voice)
- Lack of pleasure in everyday life
- Lack of ability to begin and sustain planned activities
- Speaking little, even when forced to interact.

People with negative symptoms need help with everyday tasks. They often neglect basic personal hygiene. This may make them seem lazy or unwilling to help themselves, but the problems are symptoms caused by schizophrenia. (NIMH, n.d.)

Tourette's Syndrome (TS)

According to the National Institute of Neurological Disorders and Stroke (NINDS), Tourette's syndrome (TS) is a

neurological disorder characterized by repetitive, stereotyped, involuntary movements and vocalizations called tics. The disorder is named for Dr. Georges Gilles de la Tourette, the pioneering French neurologist who in 1885 first described the condition in an 86-year-old French noblewoman.

The early symptoms of TS are almost always noticed first in childhood, with the average onset between the ages of 7 and 10 years. TS occurs in people from all ethnic groups; males are affected about three to four times more often than females. It is estimated that 200,000 Americans have the most severe form of TS, and as many as one in 100 exhibit milder and less complex symptoms such as chronic motor or vocal tics or transient tics of childhood. Although TS can be a chronic condition with symptoms lasting a lifetime, most people with the condition experience their worst symptoms in their early teens, with improvement occurring in the late teens and continuing into adulthood.

Tics are classified as either simple or complex. Simple motor tics are sudden, brief, repetitive movements that involve a limited number of muscle groups. Some of the more common simple tics include eye blinking and other vision irregularities, facial grimacing, shoulder shrugging, and head or shoulder jerking. Simple vocalizations might include repetitive throat-clearing, sniffing, or grunting sounds. Complex tics are distinct, coordinated patterns of movements involving several muscle groups. Complex motor tics might include facial grimacing combined with a head twist and a shoulder shrug. Other complex motor tics may actually appear purposeful, including sniffing or touching objects, hopping, jumping, bending, or twisting. Simple vocal tics may include throat-clearing, sniffing or snorting, grunting, or barking. More complex vocal tics include words or phrases. Perhaps the most dramatic and disabling tics include motor movements that result in self-harm such as punching oneself in the face or vocal tics including coprolalia (uttering swear words) or echolalia (repeating the words or phrases of others). Some tics are preceded by an urge or sensation in the affected muscle group, commonly called a premonitory urge. Some with TS will describe a need to complete a tic in a certain way or a certain number of times in order to relieve the urge or decrease the sensation.

Tics are often worse with excitement or anxiety and better during calm, focused activities. Certain physical experiences can trigger or worsen tics, for example tight collars may trigger neck tics, or hearing another person sniff or throat-clear may trigger similar sounds. Tics do not go away during sleep but are often significantly diminished.

Tics come and go over time, varying in type, frequency, location, and severity. The first symptoms usually occur in the head and neck area and may progress to include muscles of the trunk and extremities. Motor tics generally precede the development of vocal tics and simple tics often precede complex tics. Most patients experience peak tic severity before the mid-teen years with improvement for the majority of patients in the late teen years and early adulthood. Approximately 10 percent of those affected have a progressive or disabling course that lasts into adulthood. (NINDS, n.d.b)

Cognitive impairments often interfere with the patient's ability to lead a normal life and earn a living. They can cause great emotional distress. As stated at the beginning of this section, working with the public in a library setting, staff members are likely to encounter any or all of the previously described mental disabilities, as well as simple learning disabilities.

LIBRARIAN 411: HELP FOR THOSE ON THE FRONTLINES

The Missouri Department of Mental Health (MDMH), with funding from Library Services and Technology Act (LSTA) Grant through the Missouri State Library, has implemented a number of projects in the state to promote library services to persons with disabilities. In the fall of 2003, the MDMH was awarded LSTA funds to "promote the use of public libraries as important resources in skills development and self determination among persons with disabilities and their advocates; assist local public libraries in offering accessible library programs and services to persons with disabilities, and provide support to Institutional Libraries and MDMH computer sites to enhance services through training and networking with local community libraries" (MDMH, 2009).

In 2005, MDMH focused on two main initiatives in two Missouri cities: "The Kansas City Public Library, in conjunction with Truman Behavioral Mental Health Center, developed training materials and conducted training for the Kansas City Area Library Consortia regarding providing services to persons with disabilities. [And] the Joplin Regional Center, in partnership with libraries in Joplin and other rural libraries, held several trainings which focused on assistive technology and other disability related topics. In 2006, two new sites were chosen to participate in the project. During 2006, librarians, persons with disabilities, family and other community members participated in training sponsored by the Sikeston and Daniel Boone Regional Library sites. Efforts also continued in the Joplin and Kansas City areas" (MDMH, 2009).

In 2007, "a comprehensive training curriculum for Librarians was developed. Feedback obtained from focus groups was used in the curriculum development. Focus group members included public librarians, professionals, and people with disabilities . . . The LSTA training curriculum was completed in the fall of 2007. The training includes modules regarding disability awareness, disability etiquette, assistive technology and crisis response. It was piloted at the Missouri Library Association conference in Springfield in the October 2007" (MDMH, 2009).

The 2007 LSTA Training Curriculum for librarians may be found at: http://www.librarian411.org. According to the Librarian411.org Web site: "This library training has been developed to help front-line library workers better serve patrons with mental illness and/or developmental disabilities. The training was created using input from focus groups consisting of public library staff members, mental health consumers and mental health professionals. The content of the program reflects many hours of collaboration and interaction between Department of Mental Health (DMH) librarians and the 'in-the-trenches' front-line workers of many Missouri libraries" (MDMH, 2007).

The training includes an online video series, with segments titled "Assistive Technology," "Every Fifth Customer," "Disability Etiquette," and "When Bad Things Happen to Good Librarians." In "Every Fifth Customer," viewers learn that one in five people have some form of mental illness and that mental illness isn't always recognizable or that behaviors which we might attribute to mental illness are caused by something else, such as a physical ailment or medication. This video teaches librarians to do the following:

- Ask patrons who appear to be disoriented or without direction if they need help.
- Report significant behaviors, such as discarding medications, to caregivers, when possible.
- Refer caregivers to available resources in the library and community.
- Deal with excessively demanding patrons or elderly with signs of Alzheimer's.
- Show respect at all times for all types of patrons.

PREPARED FOR ANYTHING

In "When Bad Things Happen to Good Librarians," in the Librarian 411 series, Allan Nellis, of Fulton State Hospital in Fulton, Missouri, offers tips and pointers about crisis management and response:

- The triggering event, which is not always visible, can be real or imagined, but most often results in feelings of being misunderstood or disrespected.
- The escalation phase, or the best time to diffuse a situation, has signs of escalation including raising the voice, cursing, and changes in the person's perception of personal space.
- The best response to escalating behavior is calm and firm yet respectful. Keep body language nonconfrontational, maintain eye contact, and keep distance between yourself and the other individual. Always be aware of an escape route and look for coworkers who can assist you. Move others out of the area, when feasible.

- Practice safety first. Call for help if you need it, including the assistance of local authorities.
- In an escalating or crisis situation, practice the rule of five. Use short words of five letters or less and short sentences of five words or less (e.g., "Sir, please calm down now," or "Miss, lower your voice, please").
- Don't forget that if there is a *true crisis* in the workplace, recovery and postcrisis counseling is recommended for your staff.
- Don't be afraid to ask for help.

Until you have developed your own similar list, you might wish to share this list with your staff and volunteers and have them know where to find it easily in case a crisis begins. The previous section describes a program offered in one state. You should check with your state library and the department of mental health in your state to see if a similar program is offered there.

LEARNING DISABILITIES

"What are learning disabilities? Learning disabilities are disorders that affect the ability to understand or use spoken or written language, do mathematical calculations, coordinate movements, or direct attention" (NINDS, n.d.a). "Fifteen to 20 percent of the population has learning disabilities, which affect language, spoken or written. While generally highly intelligent, these individuals experience impairments in listening, thinking, speaking, reading, writing, spelling, and doing mathematic calculations. Yet, unlike other more obvious disabilities, learning disabilities, including dyslexia and perceptual handicaps, are invisible and often go undiagnosed. . . . Reading letters backward, confusing one word for another or seeing numbers and letters that are transposed can be frustrating in any situation . . . but in a library . . . it can be nightmarish" (Nakao, 2005). "Although learning disabilities occur in very young children, the disorders are usually not recognized until the child reaches school age" (NINDS, n.d.a).

"Learning disabilities can be lifelong conditions. In some people, several overlapping learning disabilities may be apparent. Other people may have a single, isolated learning problem that has little impact on their lives" (NINDS, n.d.a). While you will not be called on to diagnose or aid in the treatment of learning disabilities, it is important to be able to recognize them and understand how they might affect a person's ability to make the best use of your library's services.

Dyslexia

"Dyslexia is a brain-based type of learning disability that specifically impairs a person's ability to read. These individuals typically read at levels significantly lower than expected despite having normal intelligence [Albert Einstein was dyslexic]. Although the disorder varies from person to person, common characteristics among people with dyslexia include difficulty with spelling, phonological processing (the manipulation of sounds) and/or rapid visual-verbal responding. . . . The disability affects such a wide range of people and produces such different symptoms and varying degrees of severity that predictions are hard to make. The prognosis is generally good, however for individuals whose dyslexia is identified early, who have supportive family and friends and a strong self-image, and who are involved in a proper remediation program" (NINDS, n.d.a). An inordinate number of CEOs are dyslexic, and there is speculation that people with dyslexia have to think outside the box more often than nondyslexics.

Dyscalculia

"What is dyscalculia? Dyscalculia is a term referring to a wide range of life-long learning disabilities involving math. There is no single form of math disability, and difficulties vary from person to person and affect people differently in school and throughout life . . . Since disabilities involving math can be so different, the effects they have on a person's development can be just as different. For instance, a person who has trouble processing language will face different challenges in math than a person who has difficulty with visual-spatial relationships. Another person with trouble remembering facts and keeping a sequence of steps in order will have yet a different set of math-related challenges to overcome" (National Center for Learning Disabilities, 2009). People with dyscalculia, as well as dyslexia, might have difficulty with library call numbers, and at least one library, which we will discuss later, has created a solution for accessing its materials.

Attention Deficit Hyperactivity Disorder

"Attention Deficit Hyperactivity Disorder, ADHD, is one of the most common mental disorders that develop in children. Children with ADHD have impaired functioning in multiple settings, including home, school, and in relationships with peers. If untreated, the disorder can have long-term adverse effects into adolescence and adulthood" (NIMH, n.d.). You will probably have at least one child with ADHD at every story hour, enrolled in summer reading, or using the computer terminals on any given day in most libraries. "Signs and symptoms of ADHD will appear over the course of many months, and include:

- Impulsiveness: a child who acts quickly without thinking first.
- Hyperactivity: a child who can't sit still, walks, runs, or climbs around when others are seated, talks when others are talking.
- Inattention: a child who daydreams or seems to be in another world, is sidetracked by what is going on around him or her." (NIMH, n.d.)

"Hyperactive children always seem to be 'on the go' or constantly in motion. They dash around touching or playing with whatever is in sight, or talk incessantly. Sitting still at dinner or during a school lesson or story can be a difficult task. They squirm and fidget in their seats or roam around the room. Or they may wiggle their feet, touch everything, or noisily tap their pencil. Hyperactive teenagers or adults may feel internally restless. They often report needing to stay busy and may try to do several things at once.

Impulsive children seem unable to curb their immediate reactions or think before they act. They will often blurt out inappropriate comments, display their emotions without restraint, and act without regard for the later consequences of their conduct. Their impulsivity may make it hard for them to wait for things they want or to take their turn in games. They may grab a toy from another child or hit when they're upset. Even as teenagers or adults, they may impulsively choose to do things that have an immediate but small payoff rather than engage in activities that may take more effort yet provide much greater but delayed rewards" (NIMH, n.d.). Some signs of hyperactivity-impulsivity are:

- Feeling restless, often fidgeting with hands or feet, or squirming while seated;
- Running, climbing, or leaving a seat in situations where sitting or quiet behavior is expected;
- Blurting out answers before hearing the whole question; and
- Having difficulty waiting in line or taking turns. (U.S. Department of Health and Human Services, 2005)

"Children who are inattentive have a hard time keeping their minds on any one thing and may get bored with a task after only a few minutes. If they are doing something they really enjoy, they have no trouble paying attention. But focusing deliberate, conscious attention to organizing and completing a task or learning something new is difficult.

Homework is particularly hard for these children, [and as a result, they might end up at the local library looking for help.] They will forget to write down an assignment, or leave it at school. They will forget to bring a book home, or bring the wrong one. The homework, if finally finished, is full of errors and erasures. Homework is often accompanied by frustration for both parent and child" (NIMH, n.d.).

One library, the Oakland Public Library, is making a difference for patrons with learning disabilities. In "Oakland: Library Icons Help Those with Learning Disabilities Navigate the Shelves" (Nakao, 2005), Annie Nakao, a *San Francisco Chronicle* staff writer, documents how this library is making library use easier for those with learning disabilities. Having a learning disability can impair an individual's ability to use the library, resulting in an unhappy experience and the library's loss of a user in need of help.

The Oakland, California, Public Library received a $33,285 grant, "one of 30 awarded by the [California] state library as part of a multimillion dollar project to help public libraries improve services to people with disabilities" (Nakao, 2005).

Librarians in Oakland outfitted the library with "150 full-color pictograms, or graphic symbols, that convert the . . . Dewey decimal system into easily recognizable images for library patrons with learning disabilities. The universal access of the symbols will also help many other patrons, including those with poor vision, non-English speakers, or anyone who finds it easier to locate books using visual images. 'We hope it's going to help just about everyone, even librarians,' says resource librarian Lynne Cutler, who, as the library's disability services advocate, was the driving force behind the project" (Nakao, 2005).

Even library patrons with ADHD can benefit from the use of pictograms, as the time it takes to use the library catalog and decipher call numbers can lead to frustration and ultimately a failed attempt to locate needed materials. A volunteer at the Oakland Public Library, who has ADHD, admitted that for her "to walk into this big place with stacks of books that all look the same could be overwhelming . . . Where do I start? So these pictograms are really cool. They stand out, and they make the library much more user friendly" (Nakao, 2005). Without this or other such aids, patrons with disabilities might hide library books in places where they can find them again, or resort to various other tactics. These phenomena might explain the dislocation of some of our library materials on a regular basis.

The pictograms, "encased in plastic sleeves, aren't huge, maybe 4-by-5 inches, and jut out only slightly from bookshelves" (Nakao, 2005). While not being overly obtrusive, they are eye-catching and much less intimidating than the Dewey decimal system. The symbols are representative of various subject areas. For example, "a blue telescope, looking up into a sky spangled with Saturn, the moon, sun and stars, is the symbol for astronomy. Science fiction sports a green-and-purple spaceship, spurting flames. The African American reference section has a portrait of influential scholar and activist W.E.B. Dubois. Each pictogram is imprinted with the name of the section, and its Dewey decimal number . . . magic was pulling a rabbit out of a hat, gardening was flowers . . . [and] history . . . [is] a design incorporating pyramids with an hourglass of sand" (Nakao, 2005).

It has been suggested that "the Dewey decimal system doesn't make sense to anyone without a degree in library science" (Nakao, 2005) and that the use of something like pictograms is a less intimidating and user friendly way to make sense of library arrangement. "The pictograms are 'one more link' to help people with disabilities get full use of libraries" (Nakao, 2005). How cool is that?

In addition to the pictogram project, "the grant also paid for more Kurzweil 300 software, a reading program that enables a computer to scan a text on the Internet and read it aloud, as well as software to help middle and high school students build critical thinking and writing skills. They will add to the library's other services for those with disabilities, including video relay service for those who are deaf, and Zoomtext software that magnifies and reads information on the computer screen. Some 650 people are also enrolled in a program that extends the checkout period for materials from three to six weeks for users with disabilities . . . [in the] hopes that expanding services attract more patrons with disabilities" (Nakao, 2005). What a wonderful concept.

CONCLUSION

While dealing with patrons with mental and learning disabilities can be a difficult prospect, there are resources available to help librarians learn the specifics of these disabilities and how to deal with them effectively. Patience, however, is a virtue, and since persons with mental and learning disabilities are a part of every community, including the homeless, it is in everyone's best interest for librarians to practice patience in their daily interactions with these patrons.

CHAPTER 6

Summing It All Up

Persons with disabilities are often recognized for their disability, in much the same way that we recognize people by skin color or other physical attributes. It is important to remember that a disability does not define a person but is only a part of what makes an individual unique. People with disabilities have information needs that are as varied as the rest of the population, ranging from simple reference questions to need for computer training or assistance and, sometimes, perhaps, an unrecognized desire (and the right) to be a part of the library community. Putting the person first in dealing with persons with disabilities is the bedrock for forming policies and setting standards in your library.

By making the effort to ensure that all of your library's services and programs are accessible to those with disabilities, you embrace an often overlooked library user group. In addition to the physical accessibility of your library, you should strive for Web accessibility, which is the major source of access to your library collections and means of marketing your services. Be aware of Americans with Disabilities Act (ADA) requirements for your facility and at the very minimum do the following:

- Create a written access plan.
- Publicize your services and policies to agencies that work with persons with disabilities, just like you would to any population.
- Have a request for accommodation policy in place and make it a pleasant and easy process.

- Maintain accessible parking, clear paths of travel to and throughout the facility.
- Maintain adequate, clear openings, at least 32 inches in width, or automatic doors.
- Install handrails, ramps, and elevator.
- Install accessible tables and public service desks.
- Ensure that public conveniences such as restrooms and drinking fountains are accessible.

Physical and intellectual access options are expanding as assistive technology in libraries becomes more commonplace, but library services will only be accessible to everyone if librarians make the effort to provide that access. Librarians should base assistive technology purchases on patron needs, and when assistive equipment is not available, they must develop workarounds or adapt existing technology when possible.

If you can't afford to have several forms of adaptive technology available to your patrons, consider the following:

- Large print key labels can assist patrons with low vision.
- Software to enlarge screen images or changing the zoom on a single computer to enlarge.
- Large monitors of at least 17 inches.
- Trackball mouse and good wrist rests.

If you are unable to provide the type of assistive technology that you would like to provide because of budget constraints, understand that your staff will have to be *willing and prepared to provide additional help to patrons with disabilities*. Look into grant opportunities through your state library for Library Services and Technology Act funds and write a grant for assistive technology. Learning about your state's assistive technology program and the state or local network for the blind and physically handicapped can not only benefit your patrons but serve as a resource for you and your staff, as well.

Getting in on the ground floor through educating students of library and information technology about assistive technology and disability issues can pave the way for excellence in service to this underserved population. You may be the catalyst to talk to the dean or director of the nearest library and information science program preparing public librarians to explain the need for this.

While not exactly a specialized field, serving seniors does require some additional knowledge and training opportunities for library staff. Changes to eyesight, hearing, brain function, and other physical changes can make serving older adults in libraries a challenge. By paying careful attention to the special needs of patrons with disabilities, older adults, and youthful Baby Boomers, you can create successful programs within your library that will enhance their quality of life and ensure that learning is indeed a lifelong process. If library schools aren't providing the type of education that librarians need to serve populations with disabilities and the elderly, it is up to librarians in the field to locate educational opportunities for themselves and their staff. State library and state chapters of the American Library Association offer workshops and access to online educational opportunities all the time, so there's really no excuse!

Work with local agencies to design programs that are not only accessible to older adults and those with disabilities but are accessible to those who have hearing and vision loss, are in wheelchairs, or use service animals in their daily lives. Finding programs and services for those with disabilities in your community can be a rewarding experience. Think outside the box and plan gaming activities or offer up an opportunity to share artwork. Activities involving electronic interactive games, such as Wii bowling, are a hot ticket item, and for very good reasons, as we've already learned, in many libraries and senior centers. Offering opportunities to learn and develop new skills and become more active in the community makes your library the lifelong learning institution that it should be. Your efforts won't go unnoticed, and the rewards in providing services to an often ignored population will be many.

While dealing with patrons with mental and learning disabilities can be a difficult prospect, there are resources available to help librarians learn the specifics of these disabilities and how to deal with them effectively. Patience, however, is the greatest virtue, and since persons with mental and learning disabilities are a part of every community, including the homeless, it is in everyone's best interest for librarians to practice patience in their daily interactions with these patrons.

Persons with disabilities are a part of your local community, and they deserve to be welcomed with respect and little fanfare or commotion into your library. Don't let the arrival of someone in a wheelchair or a service dog send you or your staff into a tailspin. Not everyone likes to make a huge entrance into a room and be seen by everyone, including people with disabilities! By making sure that your library's physical facilities are accessible to everyone and by having a policy that states that your library serves everyone in your community regardless of physical or mental limitations, you will make persons with disabilities feel welcome and comfortable.

Persons with disabilities are just people. They are wives and husbands, daughters and sons, professionals and students, with varied information needs and varying degrees of knowledge about the myriad subjects and services that you offer. They have questions. They need answers. They want to be entertained and enlightened and educated and bedazzled by all that you and your library have to offer them. They want to be treated with respect and dignity. They are, after all, people first.

APPENDIX A

National Library Service State and Regional Libraries

Alabama
Regional Library
Alabama Regional Library for the Blind
  and Physically Handicapped
6030 Monticello Drive
Montgomery, AL 36130-6000
Librarian: Dana Pritchard
Telephone: (334) 213-3906
  and (334) 213-3921
Toll-free (In-state): (800) 392-5671
Fax: (334) 213-3993
E-mail: dana.pritchard@apls.
  alabama.gov
Web site: http://www.apls.state.al.us/webpages/
  services/BPH/BPHServices.htm
Hours of Operation: 8:00–5:00 M–F
Serves: Alabama (60 of 67 counties);
  Braille readers receive service from
  Utah.

Subregional Library
Library for the Blind and Handicapped
Anniston, AL 36202-0308
Serves: Calhoun County

Subregional Library
Department for the Blind and Physically
  Handicapped
Houston-Love Memorial Library
P.O. Box 1369
Dothan, AL 36302
Librarian: Christi Armstrong
Telephone: (334) 793-9767
TDD: (334) 793-9767
Fax: (334) 793-6645
E-mail: carmstrong0828@yahoo.com
Hours of Operation: 9:00–9:00, M, T, Th;
  9:00–6:00 W, F, 9:00–5:00 Sat; 1:00–5:00 Sun
Serves: Houston County

Subregional Library
Huntsville Subregional Library for the
    Blind and Physically Handicapped
P.O. Box 443
Huntsville, AL 35804
Librarian: Joyce Welch
Telephone: (256) 532-5980
    and (256) 532-5981
Fax: (256) 532-5994
E-mail: jwelch@hpl.lib.al.us
    or bphdept@hpl.lib.al.us
Web site: http://www.hpl.lib.al.us/
    departments/bph/
Hours of Operation: 8:00–4:30 M–F
Serves: Madison County

Subregional Library
Tuscaloosa Subregional Library for the
    Blind and Physically Handicapped
Tuscaloosa Public Library
1801 Jack Warner Parkway
Tuscaloosa, AL 35401
Librarian: Barbara B. Jordan
Telephone: (205) 345-3994
Fax: (205) 752-8300
E-mail: bjordan@tuscaloosa-library.org
Web site: http://www.tuscaloosa-library.
    org/pages/bph.html
Hours of Operation: 9:00–5:00 M–F
Serves: Tuscaloosa County

Subregional Library
Library and Resource Center for the Blind
    and Physically Handicapped
Alabama Institute for Deaf and Blind
705 South Street
P.O. Box 698
Talladega, AL 35161
Librarian: Teresa Lacy
Telephone: (256) 761-3237
Toll-free (In-state): (800) 848-4722
Fax: (256) 761-3561
E-mail: Lacy.Teresa@aidb.state.al.us or
    Thompson.Martha@aidb.state.al.us
Web site: http://www.aidb.org
Hours of Operation: 8:00–4:30 M–F
Serves: Coosa, St. Clair, and Talladega
    counties

Alaska
Regional Library
Alaska State Library
Talking Book Center
344 West Third Avenue, Suite 125
Anchorage, AK 99501
Librarian: Patience Frederiksen
Telephone: (907) 269-6575
Toll-free (In-state): (800) 776-6566
Fax: (907) 269-6580
E-mail: Patience.Frederiksen@alaska.gov
Web site: http://www.library.state.ak.us/dev/tbc.html
Hours of Operation: 8:00–4:30 M–F
Serves: Alaska; Braille readers receive service
    from Utah.

Arizona
Regional Library
Arizona State Braille and Talking Book Library
1030 North 32nd Street
Phoenix, AZ 85008
Librarian: Linda A Montgomery
Telephone: (602) 255-5578
Toll-free (In-state): (800) 255-5578
Fax: (602) 286-0444
E-mail: btbl@lib.az.us
Web site: http://www.lib.az.us/braille/
Hours of Operation: 8:00–5:00 M–F
Serves: Arizona; Braille readers receive
    service from Utah.

Arkansas
Regional Library
Library for the Blind and Physically Handicapped
One Capitol Mall
Little Rock, AR 72201-1085
Librarian: John D. Hall
Telephone: (501) 682-1155
Toll-free (In-state): (866) 660-0885
TDD: (501) 682-1002
Fax: (501) 682-1529
E-mail: nlsbooks@asl.lib.ar.us
Web site: http://www.asl.lib.ar.us/ASLBPH.htm
Hours of Operation: 8:00–5:00 M–F
Serves: Arkansas

Subregional Library
Library for the Blind and Handicapped,
    Southwest

Columbia County Library
220 East Main Street
P.O. Box 668
Magnolia, AR 71754
Librarian: Sandra Grissom
Telephone: (870) 234-0399
Toll-free (In-state): (866) 234-8273
Fax: (870) 234-5077
E-mail: lbph@hotmail.com
Hours of Operation: 9:00–5:00 M–F
Serves: Bradley, Calhoun, Cleveland,
    Columbia, Dallas, Hempstead, Howard,
    Lafayette, Little River, Miller, Nevada,
    Ouachita, Pike, Polk, Sevier, and Union
    counties

California
Regional Library
Braille and Talking Book Library
California State Library
P.O. Box 942837
Sacramento, CA 94237-0001
Librarian: Mike L Marlin
Telephone: (916) 654-0640
Toll-free (In-state): (800) 952-5666
Fax: (916) 654-1119
E-mail: btbl@library.ca.gov
Web site: http://www.btbl.ca.gov
Hours of Operation: 9:30–4:00 M–F
Serves: Northern California

Regional Library
Braille Institute
Library Services
741 North Vermont Avenue
Los Angeles, CA 90029-3594
Librarian: Henry C. Chang
Telephone: (323) 663-1111
    and (323) 660-3880
Toll-free (In-state): (800) 808-2555
TDD: (323) 660-3880
Fax: (323) 662-2440
E-mail: dls@braillelibrary.org
Web site: http://www.braillelibrary.org/
Hours of Operation: 8:30–5:00 M–F
Serves: Imperial, Kern, Los Angeles, Orange,
    Riverside, San Bernardino, San Diego,
    San Luis Obispo, Santa Barbara, and Ventura
    counties

Subregional Library
Talking Book Library for the Blind
Fresno County Public Library
Ted Wills Community Center
770 North San Pablo Avenue
Fresno, CA 93728-3640
Librarian: Wendy Eisenberg
Telephone: (559) 488-3217
Toll-free (In-state): (800) 742-1011
TDD: (559) 488-1642
Fax: (559) 488-1971
E-mail: wendy.eisenberg@fresnolibrary.org
Web site: http://www.fresnolibrary.org/tblb
Hours of Operation: 9:30–5:30 M–F
Serves: Fresno, Kings, Madera, and Tulare counties

Subregional Library
Library for the Blind and Print Disabled
San Francisco Public Library
Civic Center
100 Larkin Street
San Francisco, CA 94102
Librarian: Martin Magid
Telephone: (415) 557-4253
Fax: (415) 557-4375
E-mail: lbpd@sfpl.org or mmagid@sfpl.org
Web site: http://sfpl.org/librarylocations/
    accessservices/lbpd.htm
Hours of Operation: 1:00–6:00 M, Th;
    10:00–6:00 T, W; 12:00–6:00 F
Serves: San Francisco

Colorado
Regional Library
Colorado Talking Book Library
180 Sheridan Boulevard
Denver, CO 80226-8097
Librarian: Debbi MacLeod
Telephone: (303) 727-9277
Toll-free (In-state): (800) 685-2136
Fax: (303) 727-9281
E-mail: ctbl.info@cde.state.co.us
Web site: http://www.cde.state.co.us/ctbl
Hours of Operation: 8:00–5:00 M–F
Serves: Colorado

Connecticut
Regional Library
Connecticut State Library

Library for the Blind and Physically
   Handicapped
198 West Street
Rocky Hill, CT 06067
Librarian: Carol A. Taylor
Telephone: (860) 721-2020
Toll-free (In-state): (800) 842-4516
Fax: (860) 721-2056
E-mail: lbph@cslib.org
Web site: http://www.cslib.org/lbph.htm
Hours of Operation: 9:00–3:00 M–F
Serves: Connecticut

Delaware
Regional Library
Delaware Division of Libraries
Library for the Blind and Physically
   Handicapped
43 South DuPont Highway
Dover, DE 19901
Librarian: John Phillos
Telephone: (302) 739-4748
Toll-free (In-state): (800) 282-8676
TDD: (302) 739-4748
Fax: (302) 739-6787
E-mail: john.phillos@state.de.us or
   debph@lib.de.us
Web site: http://www.state.lib.de.us/
   Collection_Development/LBPH/
Hours of Operation: 8:00–4:30 M–F
Serves: Delaware; Braille readers receive
   service from Philadelphia,
   Pennsylvania.

District of Columbia
Regional Library
Adaptive Services Division
DC Public Library
901 G Street NW
Room 215
Washington, DC 20001
Librarian: Venetia V. Demson
Telephone: (202) 727-2142
   and (202) 727-2270
TDD: (202) 727-2255
Fax: (202) 727-1129
E-mail: lbph.dcpl@dc.gov
Web site: http://www.dclibrary.org
Hours of Operation: 9:30–5:30 M–F

Serves: District of Columbia; Braille readers
   receive service from Massachusetts.

Regional Library
Network Services Section
National Library Service for the Blind and
   Physically Handicapped
Library of Congress
Washington, DC 20542
Librarian: Yealuri Rathan Raj
Telephone: (202) 707-9261
TDD: (202) 707-0744
Fax: (202) 707-0712
E-mail: raj@loc.gov or nls@loc.gov
Web site: http://www.loc.gov/nls
Hours of Operation: 8:00–4:30 M–F

Regional Library
Music Section
National Library Service for the Blind
   and Physically Handicapped
Library of Congress
Washington, DC 20542
Librarian: John Hanson
Telephone: (202) 707-9257 and (202) 707-9254
Toll-free (In-state): (800) 424-8567
TDD: (202) 707-0744
Fax: (202) 707-0712
E-mail: nlsm@loc.gov
Web site: http://www.loc.gov/nls/music/
   index.html
Hours of Operation: 8:00–4:30 M–F
Serves: All patrons interested in Braille or
   large-print musical scores or instructional
   music recordings.

Florida
Regional Library
Florida Bureau of Braille and Talking Book
   Library Services
421 Platt Street
Daytona Beach, FL 32114-2803
Librarian: Michael Gunde
Telephone: (386) 239-6000
Toll-free (In-state): (800) 226-6075
Fax: (386) 239-6069
E-mail: mike.gunde@dbs.fldoe.org
Web site: http://dbs.myflorida.com/library/
   index.php

Hours of Operation: 8:00–5:00 M–F
Serves: Florida

Subregional Library
Talking Books/Special Needs Library
Jacksonville Public Library
303 North Laura Street
Jacksonville, FL 32202
Librarian: Jonathan A. Reynolds
Telephone: (904) 630-1999 and (904) 630-0344
Fax: (904) 630-0604
E-mail: jerryr@coj.net
Web site: http://jpl.coj.net/lib/talkingbooks.
   html
Hours of Operation: 9:00–5:00 M–F
Serves: Duval County

Subregional Library
Talking Books Library
Miami-Dade Public Library System
2455 NW 183rd Street
Miami, FL 33056-3641
Librarian: Barbara L. Moyer
Telephone: (305) 751-8687
Toll-free (In-state): (800) 451-9544
TDD: (305) 474-7258
Fax: (305) 757-8401
E-mail: moyerb@mdpls.org or
   talkingbooks@mdpls.org
Web site: http://www.mdpls.org/services/
   outreach/talk_books.asp
Hours of Operation: 8:30–5:00 M–F
Serves: Miami-Dade and Monroe counties

Subregional Library
Orange County Library System
Talking Book Section
101 East Central Boulevard
Orlando, FL 32801
Librarian: Lelia Higgins
Telephone: (407) 835-7464
TDD: (407) 835-7641
Fax: (407) 835-7642
E-mail: higgins.lelia@ocls.info
Web site: http://www.ocls.info/About/
   assistiveServices.asp
Hours of Operation: 9:00–9:00 M–Th;
   9:00–6:00 F, Sat; 1:00–6:00 Sun
Serves: Orange County

Subregional Library
Manatee Talking Book Library
Bradenton, FL 34207
Serves: Manatee and Sarasota counties

Subregional Library
Hillsborough County Talking Book Library
Jan Kaminis Platt Regional Library
3910 South Manhattan Avenue
Tampa, FL 33611-1214
Librarian: Ann Palmer
Telephone: (813) 272-6024
TDD: (813) 272-6305
Fax: (813) 272-6072
E-mail: talkingbooks@hillsboroughcounty.org
Web site: http://hcplc.org/hcplc/liblocales/tbl
Hours of Operation: 10:00–5:00 M–F
Serves: Hillsborough County

Subregional Library
Talking Books
Palm Beach County Library Annex
Mil-Lake Plaza
4639 Lake Worth Road
Lake Worth, FL 33463
Librarian: Pat Mistretta
Telephone: (561) 649-5500
Toll-free (In-state): (888) 780-5151
Fax: (561) 649-5402
E-mail: talkingbooks@pbclibrary.org
Web site: http://www.pbclibrary.org/
   outreach-talkingbooks.htm
Hours of Operation: 9:00–5:00 M–F
Serves: Palm Beach County

Subregional Library
Broward County Talking Book Library
100 South Andrews Avenue
Ft. Lauderdale, FL 33301
Librarian: Wayne Draper
Telephone: (954) 357-7555 and (954) 357-8686
TDD: (954) 357-7528
Fax: (954) 357-7420
E-mail: wdraper@browardlibrary.org or
   talkingbooks@browardlibrary.org
Web site: http://www.broward.org/library/
   talkingbooks.htm
Hours of Operation: 9:00–5:00 M–F
Serves: Broward County

Subregional Library
Lee County Talking Books Library
13240 North Cleveland Avenue, #5–6
North Ft. Myers, FL 33903-4855
Librarian: Sheldon Kaye
Telephone: (239) 995-2665
Toll-free (In-state): (800) 854-8195
TDD: (239) 995-2665
Fax: (239) 995-1681
E-mail: talkingbooks@leegov.com
Web site: http://www.lee-county.com/
   library/progserv/ssvcs/tb.htm
Hours of Operation: 8:30–5:00 M–F
Serves: Lee County

Subregional Library
Brevard County Libraries
Talking Books Library
308 Forrest Avenue
Cocoa, FL 32922-7781
Librarian: Debra A. Martin
Telephone: (321) 633-1810 and (321) 633-1811
TDD: (321) 633-1838
Fax: (321) 633-1838
E-mail: dmartin@brev.org
Web site: http://www.brev.org/about_bcl/
   disabled_services.htm
Hours of Operation: 9:00–5:00 M–F
Serves: Brevard County

Subregional Library
West Florida Public Library
Talking Book Library
200 West Gregory Street
Pensacola, FL 32502-4822
Librarian: Susan C. Voss
Telephone: (850) 436-5065 and (850) 436-5060
Fax: (850) 436-5039
E-mail: talkingbooks@ci.pensacola.fl.us or
   svoss@ci.pensacola.fl.us
Web site: http://www.cityofpensacola.com/
   library/page.asp?pid=5037
Hours of Operation: 9:00–4:00 M–F
Serves: Escambia County (no longer serving
   Santa Rosa County)

Subregional Library
Pinellas Talking Book Library
1330 Cleveland Street

Clearwater, FL 33755-5103
Librarian: Marilyn Stevenson
Telephone: (727) 441-9958
Toll-free (In-state): (866) 619-9568
TDD: (727) 441-3168
Fax: (727) 441-9068
E-mail: mstevenson@pplc.us
Web site: http://www.pplc.us/tbl/
Hours of Operation: 9:00–4:30 M–F
Serves: Pinellas County, Manatee County,
   Sarasota County

Georgia
Regional Library
Georgia Library for Accessible Services (GLASS)
1150 Murphy Avenue SW
Atlanta, GA 30310
Librarian: Stella Cone
Telephone: (404) 756-4619 and (404) 756-4476
Toll-free (In-state): (800) 248-6701
Fax: (404) 756-4618
E-mail: glass@georgialibraries.org or
   bwilliams@georgialibraries.org
Web site: http://www.georgialibraries.org/
   public/glass.html
Hours of Operation: 8:00–5:00 M–F
Serves: Georgia; Braille readers receive
   service from Utah.

Subregional Library
Albany Library for the Blind and Physically
   Handicapped
Dougherty County Public Library
300 Pine Avenue
Albany, GA 31701
Librarian: Kathryn R. Sinquefield
Telephone: (229) 420-3220
Toll-free (In-state): (800) 337-6251
Fax: (229) 420-3240
E-mail: lbph@docolib.org
Web site: http://www.docolib.org/libblind.html
Hours of Operation: 9:30–6:00 M–F
Serves: Calhoun, Clay, Crisp, Dooly, Dougherty,
   Lee, Randolph, Schley, Sumter, Terrell, and
   Webster counties

Subregional Library
Special Needs Library of Northeast Georgia
Athens-Clarke County Regional Library

2025 Baxter Street
Athens, GA 30606-6331
Librarian: Claudia L. Markov
Librarian: Pete Hayek
Telephone: (706) 613-3655
Toll-free (In-state): (800) 531-2063
TDD: (706) 613-3655
Fax: (706) 613-3660
E-mail: specialneedslibrary@athenslibrary.org
Web site: http://www.clarke.public.lib.ga.us/
    specneeds/index.html
Hours of Operation: 9:00–6:00 M–F
Serves: Banks, Barrow, Clarke, Elbert, Franklin,
    Greene, Gwinnett, Habersham, Hancock, Hart,
    Jackson, Jasper, Madison, Morgan, Oconee,
    Oglethorpe, Putnam, Rabun, Stephens, Walton,
    and White counties

Subregional Library
Talking Book Center
Augusta Regional Library
425 James Brown Boulevard
Augusta, GA 30901
Librarian: Gary Swint
Telephone: (706) 821-2625
Fax: (706) 724-5403
E-mail: talkbook@ecgrl.org
Web site: http://www.ecgrl.public.lib.ga.us/
    lbph.htm
Hours of Operation: 9:00–7:00 M–Th;
    9:00–5:30 F, Sat
Serves: Burke, Columbia, Jefferson, Lincoln,
    McDuffie, Richmond, Taliafferro, Warren,
    and Wilkes counties

Subregional Library
Bainbridge Subregional Library for the Blind
    and Physically Handicapped
Southwest Georgia Regional Library
301 South Monroe Street
Bainbridge, GA 39819-4029
Librarian: Susan S. Whittle
Telephone: (229) 248-2680
Toll-free (In-state): (800) 795-2680
TDD: (229) 248-2665
Fax: (229) 248-2670
E-mail: lbph@swgrl.org
Web site: http://www.swgrl.org/local/lbph/
    LBPH1.HTM

Hours of Operation: 8:30–5:30 M–F
Serves: Baker, Brooks, Colquitt, Decatur,
    Early, Grady, Miller, Mitchell, Seminole,
    Thomas, and Worth counties

Subregional Library
Columbus Library for Accessible Services
    (CLASS)
The Columbus Public Library
3000 Macon Road
Columbus, GA 31906-2201
Librarian: Suzanne Barnes
Telephone: (706) 243-2686 and (706) 243-2688
Toll-free (In-state): (800) 652-0782
Fax: (706) 243-2710
E-mail: sbarnes@cvrls.net
Web site: http://www.thecolumbuslibrary.org/
    outreachservices/class.html
Hours of Operation: 9:00–5:00 M–F
Serves: Chattahoochee, Coweta, Harris, Marion,
    Meriwether, Muscogee, Stewart, Talbot, Taylor,
    Troup, and Upson counties

Subregional Library
Oconee Regional Library
Library for the Blind and Physically Handicapped
801 Bellevue Avenue
P.O. Box 100
Dublin, GA 31040
Librarian: Wanda Daniel
Telephone: (478) 275-5382
Toll-free (In-state): (800) 453-5541
Fax: (478) 275-3821
E-mail: wdaniel@ocrl.org
Web site: http://www.laurens.public.lib.ga.us/
    index.pl/special_service_center.html
Hours of Operation: 8:30–5:30 M–F
Serves: Bleckley, Dodge, Glascock, Johnson,
    Laurens, Montgomery, Pulaski, Tattnall,
    Telfair, Toombs, Treutlen, Washington,
    Wheeler, and Wilcox counties

Subregional Library
Hall County Library System
Gainesville Subregional LBPH
East Hall Branch and Special Needs Library
2434 Old Cornelia Highway
Gainesville, GA 30507
Librarian: Adrian Mixson

Telephone: (770) 532-3311
TDD: (770) 531-2530
Fax: (770) 531-2502
E-mail: amixson@hallcountylibrary.org
Web site: http://www.hallcountylibrary.org/
    ehmap.htm
Hours of Operation: 10:00–7:00 M–Th;
    10:00–5:00 F
Serves: Hall County

Subregional Library
North Georgia Talking Book Center
LaFayette, GA 30728
Serves: Catoosa, Chattooga, Dade, Fannin,
    Gordon, Murray, Towns, Union, Walker,
    and Whitfield counties

Subregional Library
Middle Georgia Subregional Library
    for the Blind and Physically Handicapped
Washington Memorial Library
1180 Washington Avenue
Macon, GA 31201-1790
Librarian: Judy T. Harrington
Telephone: (478) 744-0877
Toll-free (In-state): (800) 805-7613
TDD: (478) 744-0877
Fax: (478) 744-0840
E-mail: harringj@bibblib.org
Web site: http://www.co.bibb.ga.us/library/TBC.htm
Hours of Operation: 9:00–5:00 M–F
Serves: Baldwin, Bibb, Crawford, Houston, Jones,
    Macon, Peach, Twiggs, and Wilkinson counties

Subregional Library
Rome Subregional Library for People with
    Disabilities
Sara Hightower Regional Library
205 Riverside Parkway NE
Rome, GA 30161-2911
Librarian: Delana Hickman
Telephone: (706) 236-4618 and (706) 236-4615
Toll-free (In-state): (888) 263-0769
TDD: (706) 236-4618
Fax: (706) 236-4631
E-mail: dhickman@rome-lpd.org or
    btreadaway@rome-lpd.org
Web site: http://www.rome-lpd.org
Hours of Operation: 8:30–4:30 M–F

Serves: Bartow, Carroll, Cherokee,
    Douglas, Floyd, Gilmer, Haralson, Heard,
    Paulding, Pickens, and Polk counties

Subregional Library
Subregional Library for the Blind
    and Physically Handicapped
Live Oak Public Libraries
Thunderbolt Branch
2708 Mechanics Avenue
Savannah, GA 31404
Librarian: Linda Stokes
Telephone: (912) 354-5864
Toll-free (In-state): (800) 342-4455
TDD: (912) 354-5534
Fax: (912) 354-5534
E-mail: stokesl@liveoakpl.org or
    lbphsav@liveoakpl.org
Web site: http://www.liveoakpl.org/about-us/
    library-for-the-blind-physical.php
Hours of Operation: 9:00–6:00 M–F
Serves: Bryan, Bulloch, Candler, Chatham,
    Effingham, Emanuel, Evans, Jenkins,
    Liberty, and Screven counties

Subregional Library
Valdosta Talking Book Center
South Georgia Regional Library
300 Woodrow Wilson Drive
Valdosta, GA 31602-2592
Librarian: Diane Jernigan
Telephone: (229) 333-7658 and (229) 333-0086
Toll-free (In-state): (800) 246-6515
Fax: (229) 333-0774
E-mail: djernigan@sgrl.org
Hours of Operation: 9:30–5:30 M–F
Serves: Atkinson, Ben Hill, Berrien, Coffee,
    Cook, Echols, Irwin, Jeff Davis, Lanier,
    Lowndes, Tift, and Turner counties

Subregional Library
Three Rivers Regional Library
Brunswick-Glynn County Regional Library
208 Gloucester St.
Brunswick, GA 31520-5324
Librarian: Betty D. Ransom
Telephone: (912) 267-1212
Toll-free (In-state): (866) 833-2878
Fax: (912) 267-9597

E-mail: bransom@trrl.org
Hours of Operation: 9:00–5:00 M–F
Serves: Appling, Bacon, Brantley, Camden,
   Charlton, Clinch, Glynn, Long, McIntosh,
   Pierce, Ware, and Wayne counties

Subregional Library
Atlanta Metro Subregional Library
One Margaret Mitchell Square
Atlanta, GA 30303
Toll-free (In-state): (800) 248-6701
Hours of Operation: **Opening early 2010*

Guam
Subregional Library
Guam Public Library for the Blind and Physically
   Handicapped
Nieves M. Flores Memorial Library
254 Martyr Street
Agana, GU 96910
Librarian: Teresita Kennimer
Telephone: (671) 475-4753 and (671) 475-4754
Fax: (671) 477-9777
Hours of Operation: 9:30–6:00 M, W, F; 9:30–
   8:00 T, Th; 10:00–4:00 Sat; 12:00–4:00 Sun
Serves: Guam

Hawaii
Regional Library
Hawaii State Library for the Blind and Physically
   Handicapped
402 Kapahulu Avenue
Honolulu, HI 96815
Librarian: Fusako Miyashiro
Telephone: (808) 733-8444
Toll-free (In-state): (800) 559-4096
TDD: (808) 733-8444
Fax: (808) 733-8449
E-mail: olbcirc@librarieshawaii.org or
   fusako@librarieshawaii.org
Web site: http://www.librarieshawaii.org/
   locations/oahu/lbph.htm
Hours of Operation: 8:30–4:30 M–F
Serves: Hawaii, Guam, and U.S. Affiliated
   Pacific Islands

Idaho
Regional Library
Idaho Commission for Libraries Talking
   Book Service

325 West State Street
Boise, ID 83702-6072
Librarian: Sue Walker
Telephone: (208) 334-2150
Toll-free (In-state): (800) 458-3271
TDD: (800) 377-1363
Fax: (208) 334-4016
E-mail: talkingbooks@libraries.idaho.gov
Web site: http://libraries.idaho.gov/tbs
Hours of Operation: 8:00–5:00 M–F
Serves: Idaho; Braille readers receive
   service from Utah

Illinois
Regional Library
Illinois State Library Talking Book
   and Braille Service
401 East Washington
Springfield, IL 62701-1207
Librarian: Sharon Ruda
Telephone: (217) 782-9435
Toll-free (In-state): (800) 665-5576
TDD: (888) 261-7863
Fax: (217) 558-4723
E-mail: sruda@ilsos.net or Psalamon@ilsos.net
Web site: http://www.ilbph.org
Hours of Operation: 8:00–4:30 M–F
Serves: Illinois; adult Braille readers receive
   service from Utah.

Subregional Library
Southern Illinois Talking Book Center
Shawnee Library System
607 South Greenbriar Road
Carterville, IL 62918-1600
Librarian: Diana Brawley Sussman
Telephone: (618) 985-8375
Toll-free (In-state): (800) 455-2665
TDD: (618) 985-8375
Fax: (618) 985-4211
E-mail: bphdcpt@shawls.lib.il.us or
   dbrawley@shawls.lib.il.us
Web site: http://www.shawls.lib.il.us/talkingbooks
Hours of Operation: 8:00–5:00 M–F
Serves: Alexander, Bond, Clay, Clinton,
   Crawford, Edward, Effingham, Fayette,
   Franklin, Gallatin, Hamilton, Hardin,
   Jackson, Jasper, Jefferson, Johnson, Lawrence,
   Madison, Marion, Massac, Monroe, Perry,

Pope, Pulaski, Randolph, Richland, Saint Clair, Saline, Union, Wabash, Washington, Wayne, White, and Williamson counties

Subregional Library
Voices of Vision
Talking Book Center
DuPage Library System
127 South First Street
Geneva, IL 60134
Librarian: Karen Odean
Telephone: (630) 208-0398
Toll-free (In-state): (800) 227-0625
Fax: (630) 208-0399
E-mail: vovinfo@dupagels.lib.il.us or kodean@dupagels.lib.il.us
Web site: http://www.vovtbc.org
Hours of Operation: 8:30–5:00 M–F
Serves: Boone, DeKalb, DuPage, Grundy, Kane, Kankakee, Kendall, Lake, LaSalle, McHenry, and Will counties and parts of Cook County

Subregional Library
Mid-Illinois Talking Book Center
Alliance Library System
600 High Point Lane, Suite 2
East Peoria, IL 61611
Librarian (acting): Lori Bell
Telephone: (309) 694-9739
Toll-free (In-state): (800) 426-0709
Fax: (309) 694-9230
E-mail: lbell@alliancelibrarysystem.com
Web site: http://www.alliancelibrarysystem.com/indexMITBC.cfm
Hours of Operation: 8:00–5:00 M–F
Serves: Adams, Brown, Bureau, Calhoun, Carroll, Cass, Champaign, Christian, Clark, Coles, Cumberland, DeWitt, Douglas, Edgar, Ford, Fulton, Greene, Hancock, Henderson, Henry, Iroquois, Jersey, Jo Daviess, Knox, Lee, Livingston, Logan, Macon, Macoupin, Marshall, Mason, McDonough, McLean, Menard, Mercer, Montgomery, Morgan, Moultrie, Ogle, Peoria, Piatt, Pike, Putnam, Rock Island, Sangamon, Schuyler, Scott, Shelby, Stark, Stephenson, Tazewell, Vermillion, Warren, Whiteside, Winnebago, and Woodford counties

Subregional Library
Chicago Public Library
Talking Book Center
400 South State Street
Fifth Floor North
Chicago, IL 60605-1203
Librarian: Deborah Taylor
Telephone: (312) 747-4001 and (312) 747-1616
Toll-free (In-state): (800) 757-4654
Fax: (312) 747-1609
E-mail: dtaylor@chipublib.org
Web site: http://www.chipublib.org/branch/details/library/harold-washington/p/Tbc/
Hours of Operation: 9:00–5:00 M, W, Sat; 11:00–7:00 T, Th
Serves: Chicago

Indiana
Regional Library
Indiana State Library
Indiana Talking Book and Braille Library
140 North Senate Avenue
Indianapolis, IN 46204
Librarian: Lissa Shanahan
Telephone: (317) 232-3684
Toll-free (In-state): (800) 622-4970
TDD: (317) 232-7763
Fax: (317) 232-3728
E-mail: lbph@library.in.gov or lshanahan@library.in.gov
Web site: http://www.in.gov/library/tbbl.htm
Hours of Operation: 8:00–4:30 M–F
Serves: Indiana

Subregional Library
Bartholomew County Public Library
536 Fifth Street
Columbus, IN 47201
Librarian: Sharon D Thompson
Telephone: (812) 379-1277
Toll-free (In-state): (800) 685-0524
Fax: (812) 379-1275
E-mail: talkingbooks@barth.lib.in.us
Web site: http://www.barth.lib.in.us/talkingbooks.html
Hours of Operation: 8:30–5:00 M–F
Serves: Bartholomew, Clark, Crawford, Decatur, Floyd, Harrison, Jackson, Jefferson, Jennings, Scott, and Washington counties

Subregional Library
Northwest Indiana Subregional Library
  for the Blind and Physically Handicapped
Lake County Public Library
1919 West 81st Avenue
Merrillville, IN 46410-5382
Librarian: Renee Lewis
Telephone: (219) 769-3541
TDD: (219) 769-3541
Fax: (219) 769-0690
E-mail: rlewis@lakeco.lib.in.us
Web site: http://www.lakeco.lib.in.us/
  talking_books.htm
Hours of Operation: 8:00–4:00 M–F
Serves: Jasper, Lake, LaPorte, Newton,
  and Porter counties

Subregional Library
Talking Books Service
Evansville-Vanderburgh Public Library
200 SE Martin Luther King Jr. Boulevard
Evansville, IN 47713-1802
Librarian: Barbara Shanks
Telephone: (812) 428-8235
Toll-free (In-state): (866) 645-2536
Fax: (812) 428-8215
E-mail: tbs@evpl.org or barbs@evpl.org
Web site: http://www.evpl.org/services/
  talkingbooks/
Hours of Operation: 8:00–5:00 M–F
Serves: Daviess, Dubois, Gibson, Knox,
  Martin, Perry, Pike, Posey, Spencer,
  Vanderburgh, and Warrick counties

Iowa
Regional Library
Library for the Blind and Physically Handicapped
Iowa Department for the Blind
524 Fourth Street
Des Moines, IA 50309-2364
Librarian: Tracey Morsek
Telephone: (515) 281-1333
Toll-free (In-state): (800) 362-2587
TDD: (515) 281-1355
Fax: (515) 281-1378
E-mail: library@blind.state.ia.us
Web site: http://www.blind.state.ia.us/library/
Hours of Operation: 8:00–5:00 M–F
Serves: Iowa

Kansas
Regional Library
Kansas State Library
Kansas Talking Books Regional Library
ESU Memorial Union
1200 Commercial, Box 4055
Emporia, KS 66801-5087
Librarian: Toni Harrell
Telephone: (620) 341-6280
Toll-free (In-state): (800) 362-0699
Fax: (620) 341-6289
E-mail: tonih@kslib.info
Web site: http://www.kslib.info/talking
Hours of Operation: 8:00–5:00 M–F
Serves: All of Kansas, with full direct
  services to Barber, Butler, Cowley, Harper,
  Harvey, Kingman, Kiowa, McPherson, Pratt,
  Reno, Rice, Stafford, and Sumner counties;
  Braille readers receive service from Utah.

Subregional Library
Western Kansas Talking Books
Northwest Kansas Library System
2 Washington Square
Norton, KS 67654-0446
Librarian: Clarice Howard
Telephone: (785) 877-5148
Toll-free (In-state): (800) 432-2858
TDD: (785) 877-5148
Fax: (785) 877-5697
E-mail: tbook@ruraltel.net
Web site: http://www.skyways.
  org/nwkls/wktb/bph.html
Hours of Operation: 8:00–5:00 M–F
Serves: Cheyenne, Clark, Comanche, Decatur,
  Edwards, Finney, Ford, Gove, Graham, Grant,
  Gray, Greeley, Hamilton, Haskell, Hodgeman,
  Kearny, Lane, Logan, Meade, Morton, Ness,
  Norton, Rawlin, Scott, Seward, Sheridan,
  Sherman, Stanton, Stevens, Thomas, Trego,
  Wallace, and Wichita counties

Subregional Library
Talking Book Service
CKLS Headquarters
1409 Williams
Great Bend, KS 67530
Librarian: Joanita Doll-Masden
Telephone: (620) 792-2393

Toll-free (In-state): (800) 362-2642
Fax: (620) 792-5495
E-mail: jmasden@ckls.org
Web site: http://www.skyways.org/KSL/
    talking/ckls.html
Hours of Operation: 8:00–5:00 M–F
Serves: Barton, Cloud, Ellis, Ellsworth, Jewell,
    Lincoln, Mitchell, Osborne, Ottawa, Pawnee,
    Phillips, Republic, Rooks, Rush, Russell,
    Saline, and Smith counties

Subregional Library
Talking Books Service
Manhattan Public Library
North Central Kansas Libraries System
629 Poyntz Avenue
Manhattan, KS 66502-6086
Librarian: Ann Pearce
Telephone: (785) 776-4741
Fax: (785) 776-1545
E-mail: annp@manhattan.lib.ks.us or
    suec@manhattan.lib.ks.us
Web site: http://www.manhattan.lib.ks.
    us/bph.html
Hours of Operation: 8:00–5:00 M–F
Serves: Chase, Clay, Dickinson, Geary, Lyon,
    Marion, Marshall, Morris, Pottawatomie,
    Riley, Wabaunsee, and Washington counties

Subregional Library
Talking Books
Topeka and Shawnee County Public Library
1515 SW 10th Ave
Topeka, KS 66604-1374
Librarian: Suzanne Bundy
Telephone: (785) 580-4530
Toll-free (In-state): (800) 432-2925
TDD: (785) 580-4545
Fax: (785) 580-4430
E-mail: tbooks@tscpl.org
Web site: http://www.tscpl.org/tbooks
Hours of Operation: 9:00–5:00 M–F
Serves: Atchison, Brown, Doniphan,
    Douglas, Franklin, Jackson, Jefferson, Johnson,
    Leavenworth, Miami, Nemaha, Osage,
    Shawnee, and Wyandotte counties

Subregional Library
Wichita Public Library

Talking Books Section
223 South Main
Wichita, KS 67202
Librarian: Brad Reha
Telephone: (316) 261-8500 and (316) 261-8574
Toll-free (In-state): (800) 362-2869
TDD: (316) 262-3972
Fax: (316) 262-4540
E-mail: breha@wichita.gov
Hours of Operation: 10:00–5:00 M–F
Serves: Allen, Anderson, Bourbon, Chautauqua,
    Cherokee, Coffey, Crawford, Elk, Greenwood,
    Labette, Linn, Montgomery, Neosho,
    Sedgwick, Wilson, and Woodson counties

Kentucky
Regional Library
Kentucky Talking Book Library
300 Coffee Tree Road
P.O. Box 537
Frankfort, KY 40602-0537
Librarian: Barbara Penegor
Telephone: (502) 564-8300
Toll-free (In-state): (800) 372-2968
Fax: (502) 564-5773
E-mail: ktbl.mail@ky.gov or
    barbara.penegor@ky.gov
Web site: http://www.kdla.ky.gov/
    collectionsktbl.htm
Hours of Operation: 8:00–4:30 M–F
Serves: Kentucky (112 of 120 counties)

Subregional Library
Louisville Talking Book Library
Louisville, KY 40203
Serves: City of Louisville and Jefferson County

Subregional Library
Northern Kentucky Talking Book Library
502 Scott Boulevard
Covington, KY 41011-1530
Librarian: Clif Mayhugh
Telephone: (859) 962-4095
Toll-free (In-state): (866) 491-7610
TDD: (859) 962-4060
Fax: (859) 962-4096
E-mail: nktbl@kentonlibrary.org
Web site: http://www.kentonlibrary.
    org/outreach/talkingbooks/index.html

Hours of Operation: 8:00–5:00 M–F
Serves: Boone, Campbell, Carroll, Gallatin,
    Grant, Kenton, Owen, and Pendleton counties

Louisiana
Regional Library
State Library of Louisiana
Services for the Blind and Physically
    Handicapped
701 North Fourth Street
Baton Rouge, LA 70802-5232
Librarian: Margaret C. Harrison
Telephone: (225) 342-4944 and (225) 342-4943
Toll-free (In-state): (800) 543-4702
Fax: (225) 342-6817
E-mail: sbph@state.lib.la.us
Web site: http://www.state.lib.la.us/
Hours of Operation: 8:00–5:00 M–F
Serves: Louisiana; Braille readers receive
    service from Utah.

Maine
Regional Library
Library Services for the Blind and Physically
    Handicapped
Maine State Library
64 State House Station
Augusta, ME 04333-0064
Librarian: Chris Boynton
Telephone: (207) 287-5650
Toll-free (In-state): (800) 762-7106
Fax: (207) 287-5654
E-mail: chrboynton@mestate.lib.me.us
Web site: http://www.maine.gov/msl/outreach
Hours of Operation: 8:00–5:00 M–F
Serves: Maine; Braille readers receive
    service from Massachusetts.

Maryland
Regional Library
Maryland State Library for the Blind
    and Physically Handicapped
415 Park Avenue
Baltimore, MD 21201-3603
Librarian: Jill Lewis
Telephone: (410) 230-2424
Toll-free (In-state): (800) 964-9209
TDD: (410) 333-8679
Fax: (410) 333-2095

E-mail: referenc@lbph.lib.md.us
Web site: http://www.lbph.lib.md.us
Hours of Operation: 8:00–5:00 M–F;
    10:00–2:00 second Sat
Serves: Maryland (except Montgomery County)

Subregional Library
Disability Resource Center
Montgomery County Department of Libraries
Rockville Library
21 Maryland Avenue, Suite 100
Rockville, MD 20850
Librarian: Francie Gilman
Telephone: (240) 777-0001 and (240) 777-0960
TDD: (240) 777-0157
E-mail: tbrq@montgomerycountymd.gov
Web site: http://www.montgomerycountymd.
    gov/apps/libraries/branchinfo/sn.asp
Hours of Operation: 9:30–8:30 M–Th;
    10:00–5:00 F; 9:00–5:00 Sat; 12:00–5:00 Sun
    during the school year.
Serves: Montgomery County

Massachusetts
Regional Library
Braille and Talking Book Library
Perkins School for the Blind
175 North Beacon Street
Watertown, MA 02472-2790
Librarian: Kim Charlson
Telephone: (617) 972-7240
Toll-free (In-state): (800) 852-3133
Fax: (617) 972-7363
E-mail: library@perkins.org or
    kim.charlson@perkins.org
Web site: http://www.perkinslibrary.org
Hours of Operation: 8:30–5:00 M–F
Serves: Massachusetts; Braille readers in District
    of Columbia, Maine, New Hampshire, Rhode
    Island, and Vermont.

Subregional Library
Talking Book Library
Worcester Public Library
3 Salem Square
Worcester, MA 01608-2074
Librarian: James Izatt
Telephone: (508) 799-1730 and (508) 799-1645
Toll-free (In-state): (800) 762-0085

TDD: (508) 799-1731
Fax: (508) 799-1676
E-mail: jizatt@cwmars.org or
　talkbook@cwmars.org
Web site: http://www.worcpublib.org/
　talkingbook/index.htm
Hours of Operation: 9:00–5:30 M–Sat;
　1:30–5:30 Sun (Oct–Apr)
Serves: Massachusetts

Michigan
Regional Library
Library of Michigan
Service for the Blind and Physically Handicapped
702 West Kalamazoo
Lansing, MI 48915-1609
Librarian: Susan Chinault
Telephone: (517) 373-5614
Toll-free (In-state): (800) 992-9012
TDD: (517) 373-1592
Fax: (517) 373-5865
E-mail: sbph@michigan.gov
Web site: http://www.michigan.gov/sbph
Hours of Operation: 9:00–5:00 T, W, F;
　1:00–5:00 M, Th
Serves: Michigan except Wayne County;
　Braille readers in all of Michigan.

Regional Library
Wayne County Regional Library for the Blind
　and Physically Handicapped
30555 Michigan Avenue
Westland, MI 48186–5310
Librarian: Maria McCarville
Telephone: (734) 727-7300
Toll-free (In-state): (888) 968-2737
TDD: (734) 727-7330
Fax: (734) 727-7333
E-mail: wcrlbph@wayneregional.lib.mi.us
Web site: http://wayneregional.lib.mi.us
Hours of Operation: 8:00–4:30 M–F
Serves: Wayne County except parts of Detroit
　and Highland Park; Braille readers receive
　service from Lansing, Michigan.

Subregional Library
Washtenaw Library for the Blind
　and Physically Disabled @ AADL
343 South Fifth Avenue

Ann Arbor, MI 48104
Librarian: Celeste B. Choate
Telephone: (734) 327-4224
Fax: (734) 327-8307
E-mail: WLBPD@aadl.org
Web site: http://wlbpd.aadl.org
Hours of Operation: 10:00–9:00 M; 9:00–9:00
　T–F; 9:00–6:00 Sat; 12:00–6:00 Sun
Serves: Washtenaw county

Subregional Library
Upper Peninsula Library for the Blind and
　Physically Handicapped
1615 Presque Isle Avenue
Marquette, MI 49855
Librarian: Suzanne Dees
Telephone: (906) 228-7697
Toll-free (In-state): (800) 562-8985
TDD: (906) 228-7697
Fax: (906) 228-5627
E-mail: uplbph@uproc.lib.mi.us
Web site: http://www.uproc.lib.mi.us/uplbph/
Hours of Operation: 8:00–5:00 M–F
Serves: Alger, Baraga, Chippewa, Delta,
　Dickerson, Gogebic, Houghton, Iron,
　Keweenaw, Luce, Mackinac, Marquette,
　Menominee, Ontonagon, and Schoolcraft
　counties

Subregional Library
Oakland County Library for the Visually
　and Physically Impaired
1200 North Telegraph, Department 482
Pontiac, MI 48341-0482
Librarian: Stacy O. Boucher-Tabor
Telephone: (248) 858-5050
Toll-free (In-state): (800) 774-4542
TDD: (248) 452-2247
Fax: (248) 858-9313
E-mail: lvpi@oakgov.com or
　boucher-tabors@oakgov.com
Web site: http://www.oakgov.com/lvpi
Hours of Operation: 8:30–5:00 M–F
Serves: Oakland County

Subregional Library
Genesee District Talking Book Center
Library for the Blind and Physically Handicapped
G-4195 West Pasadena Avenue

Flint, MI 48504-2344
Librarian: Deloris King
Telephone: (810) 732-1120
Toll-free (In-state): (866) 732-1120
Fax: (810) 732-1715
E-mail: dking@thegdl.org or
    outreach@thegdl.org
Web site: www.thegdl.org/services/tbc/index.htm
Hours of Operation: 9:00–5:00 M–F
Serves: Genesee, Lapeer, and Shiawassee counties

Subregional Library
Kent District Library for the Blind and
    Physically Handicapped
Wyoming Branch Library
3350 Michael Avenue, Southwest
Wyoming, MI 49509
Librarian: Michelle L. Daniel
Telephone: (616) 647-3985 and (616) 647-3980
Fax: (616) 249-9151
E-mail: lbphstaff@kdl.org or mdaniel@kdl.org
Web site: http://www.kdl.org/about_kdl/
    lbph/index.asp
Hours of Operation: 9:30–8:00 M–Th; 9:30–5:00 F,
    Sat; 1:00–5:00 Sun (Labor Day-Memorial Day)
Serves: Ionia, Kent, and Montcalm counties

Subregional Library
Grand Traverse Area Library for the Blind
    and Physically Handicapped
610 Woodmere Avenue
Traverse City, MI 49686-3397
Librarian: Kathy Kelto
Telephone: (231) 932-8558
Toll-free (In-state): (877) 931-8558
TDD: (231) 932-8507
Fax: (231) 932-8578
E-mail: lbph@tadl.tcnet.org
Web site: http://tadl.tcnet.org/index/lbph.htm
Hours of Operation: 9:00–5:00 M–F
Serves: Antrim, Benzie, Crawford, Grand
    Traverse, Kalkaska, Lake, Leelanau, Manistee,
    Mason, Mecosta, Missaukee, Newaygo, Oceana,
    Osceola, Roscommon, and Wexford counties

Subregional Library
St. Clair County Library
St. Clair County LBPH
210 McMorran Boulevard

Port Huron, MI 48060
Librarian: Melba J. Moss
Telephone: (810) 982-3600
Toll-free (In-state): (800) 272-8570
TDD: (810) 455-0200
Fax: (810) 987-7327
E-mail: mmoss@sccl.lib.mi.us
    or star@sccl.lib.mi.us
Web site: http://www.sccl.lib.mi.us/star.html
Hours of Operation: 8:30–5:00 M–F
Serves: Huron, Sanilac, St. Clair, and Tuscola
    counties

Subregional Library
Muskegon Area District Library for the Blind
    and Physically Handicapped
4845 Airline Road, Unit 5
Muskegon, MI 49444-4503
Librarian: Sheila D. Miller
Telephone: (231) 737-6310 and (231) 737-6256
Toll-free (In-state): (877) 569-4801
TDD: (231) 722-4103
Fax: (231) 737-6307
E-mail: mclsm@llcoop.org
Web site: http://www.madl.org
Hours of Operation: 8:00–5:00 M–F
Serves: Muskegon and Ottawa counties

Subregional Library
Macomb Library for the Blind and Physically
    Handicapped
16480 Hall Road
Clinton Township, MI 48038-1132
Librarian: Beverlee C. Babcock
Telephone: (586) 286-1580
Fax: (586) 286-0634
E-mail: macbld@libcoop.net or
    babbev@libcoop.net
Web site: http://www.libcoop.net/macspe
Hours of Operation: 9:00–5:00 M–F
Serves: Macomb County

Subregional Library
Detroit Subregional Library for the Blind
    and Physically Handicapped
Detroit Public Library
Frederick Douglass Branch
for Specialized Services
3666 Grand River Avenue

Detroit, MI 48208
Librarian: Dori Middleton
Telephone: (313) 833-5494
    and (313) 833-5497
TDD: (313) 833-5492
Fax: (313) 832-5597
E-mail: dmiddle@detroitpubliclibrary.org
Web site: http://www.detroitpubliclibrary.
    org/lbph/LBPH_index.htm
Hours of Operation: 10:00–6:00 M, W, Sat;
    12:00–8:00 T, Th
Serves: Detroit and Highland Park
    (Wayne County)

Minnesota
Regional Library
Minnesota Braille and Talking Book Library
388 SE 6th Avenue
Faribault, MN 55021-6340
Librarian: Catherine A. Durivage
Telephone: (507) 384-6780
Toll-free (In-state): (800) 722-0550
Fax: (507) 333-4832
E-mail: mn.btbl@state.mn.us or
    catherine.durivage@state.mn.us
Web site: http://education.state.mn.us/MDE/
    Learning_Support/MN_Braille_Talking_
    Book_Library/index.html
Hours of Operation: 9:00–4:00 M–F
Serves: Minnesota

Mississippi
Regional Library
Blind and Physically Handicapped
    Library Services
Mississippi Library Commission
3881 Eastwood Drive
Jackson, MS 39211-6473
Librarian: Rahye Puckett
Telephone: (601) 432-4116
Toll-free (In-state): (800) 446-0892
Fax: (601) 432-4476
E-mail: lbph@mlc.lib.ms.us or
    rahye@mlc.lib.ms.us
Web site: http://www.mlc.lib.ms.
    us/ServicesToLibraries/BPHLS.htm
Hours of Operation: 8:00–5:00 M–F
Serves: Mississippi; Braille readers
    receive service from Utah, and recorded

below RC40,000 are mailed from
    the Alabama Regional Library

Missouri
Regional Library
Wolfner Library for the Blind and Physically
    Handicapped
P.O. Box 387
Jefferson City, MO 65102-0387
Librarian: Richard J. Smith
Telephone: (573) 751-8720
Toll-free (In-state): (800) 392-2614
TDD: (800) 347-1379
Fax: (573) 526-2985
E-mail: wolfner@sos.mo.gov or
    richard.smith@sos.mo.gov
Web site: http://www.sos.mo.gov/wolfner
Hours of Operation: 8:00–5:00 M–F
Serves: Missouri

Montana
Regional Library
Montana Talking Book Library
1515 East Sixth Avenue
P.O. Box 201800
Helena, MT 59620-1800
Librarian: Christie O. Briggs
Telephone: (406) 444-2064 and (406) 444-5399
Toll-free (In-state): (800) 332-3400
Fax: (406) 444-0266
E-mail: cbriggs@mt.gov
Web site: http://msl.mt.gov/tbl/tbl.asp
Hours of Operation: 8:00–5:00 M–F
Serves: Montana; Braille readers receive
    service from Utah.

Nebraska
Regional Library
Nebraska Library Commission
Talking Book and Braille Service
The Atrium
1200 N Street, Suite 120
Lincoln, NE 68508-2023
Librarian: David Oertli
Telephone: (402) 471-4038
Toll-free (In-state): (800) 742-7691
TDD: (402) 471-4038
Fax: (402) 471-6244
E-mail: talkingbook@nlc.state.ne.us or
    doertli@nlc.state.ne.us

Web site: http://www.nlc.state.ne.us/tbbs/
Hours of Operation: 8:00–5:00 M–F
Serves: Nebraska; Braille readers receive
    service from Utah.

Nevada
Regional Library
Nevada Talking Book Services
Nevada State Library and Archives
100 North Stewart Street
Carson City, NV 89701-4285
Librarian: Keri E. Putnam
Telephone: (775) 684-3354
Toll-free (In-state): (800) 922-9334
TDD: (775) 687-8338
Fax: (775) 684-3355
E-mail: kputnam@nevadaculture.org or
    sarnn@nevadaculture.org
Web site: http://www.nvtalkingbooks.org
Hours of Operation: 8:00–5:00 M–F
Serves: Nevada; Braille readers receive
    service from Utah.

New Hampshire
Regional Library
New Hampshire State Library
Talking Book Services
117 Pleasant Street
Concord, NH 03301-3852
Librarian: John C. Barrett
Telephone: (603) 271-3429 and (603) 271-2417
Toll-free (In-state): (800) 491-4200
Fax: (603) 271-8370
E-mail: DCR-TalkingBooks@dcr.nh.gov or
    John.Barrett@dcr.nh.gov
Web site: http://www.nh.gov/nhsl/talking_books/
Hours of Operation: 8:00–4:30 M–F
Serves: New Hampshire; Braille readers
    receive service from Massachusetts.

New Jersey
Regional Library
New Jersey Library for the Blind and
    Handicapped
P.O. Box 501
Trenton, NJ 08625-0501
Librarian: Adam Szczepaniak, Jr.
Telephone: (609) 530-4000
Toll-free (In-state): (800) 792-8322

TDD: (800) 882-5593
Fax: (609) 530–6384
E-mail: njlbh@njstatelib.org
Web site: http://www.njlbh.org/
Hours of Operation: 9:00–4:30 M–F; 9:00–3:00
Serves: New Jersey

New Mexico
Regional Library
New Mexico Library for the Blind and
    Physically Handicapped
1209 Camino Carlos Rey
Santa Fe, NM 87507-5166
Librarian: John Mugford
Telephone: (505) 476-9770 and (505) 476-9772
Toll-free (In-state): (800) 456-5515
Fax: (505) 476-9776
E-mail: lbph@state.nm.us
Web site: http://www.nmstatelibrary.org/
Hours of Operation: 9:00–5:00 M–F
Serves: New Mexico; Braille readers receive
    service from Utah.

New York
Regional Library
The New York Public Library
Andrew Heiskell Braille and Talking
Book Library
40 West 20th Street
New York, NY 10011-4211
Librarian: Mark McCluski
Telephone: (212) 206-5425 and (212) 206-5400
TDD: (212) 206-5458
Fax: (212) 206-5418
E-mail: mmccluski@nypl.org or ahlbph@nypl.org
Web site: http://talkingbooks.nypl.org//
Hours of Operation: Onsite: 10–5 M, W, F, Sat;
    12–7 T, Th; telephone: 10–5 M, W, F, Sat;
    10–7 T and Th
Serves: New York City and Long Island

Regional Library
New York State Talking Book and Braille Library
Cultural Education Center
Empire State Plaza
Albany, NY 12230
Librarian (acting): Sharon B. Phillips
Telephone: (518) 474-5935
Toll-free (In-state): (800) 342-3688

Fax: (518) 486-1957
E-mail: tbbl@mail.nysed.gov or
    tbblkids@mail.nysed.gov
Web site: http://www.nysl.nysed.gov/tbbl/
Hours of Operation: 8:00–4:30 M–F
Serves: New York State except New York City
    and Long Island

Subregional Library
Long Island Talking Book Library (LITBL)
Outreach Services
Suffolk Cooperative Library System
627 North Sunrise Service Road
P.O. Box 9000
Bellport, NY 11713-9000
Librarian: Valerie Lewis
Telephone: (631) 286-1600
Toll-free (In-state): (866) 833-1122
TDD: (631) 286-4546
Fax: (631) 286-1647
E-mail: vlewis@suffolk.lib.ny.us or
    lbph@suffolk.lib.ny.us
Web site: http://www.litbl.org
Hours of Operation: 9:00–5:00 M–F
Serves: Nassau and Suffolk counties

North Carolina
Regional Library
North Carolina Library for the Blind
    and Physically Handicapped
State Library of North Carolina
Department of Cultural Resources
1841 Capital Boulevard
Raleigh, NC 27604-2188
Librarian: Carl R. Keehn
Telephone: (919) 733-4376
Toll-free (In-state): (888) 388-2460
TDD: (919) 733-1462
Fax: (919) 733-6910
E-mail: nclbph@ncdcr.gov or
    carl.keehn@ncdcr.gov
Web site: http://statelibrary.dcr.
    state.nc.us/lbph/lbph.htm
Hours of Operation: 8:00–5:00 M–F
Serves: North Carolina

North Dakota
Regional Library
North Dakota State Library

Talking Book Services
604 East Boulevard Avenue
Department 250
Bismarck, ND 58505-0800
Librarian: Susan B. Hammer-Schneider
Telephone: (701) 328-2185 and (701) 328-1408
Toll-free (In-state): (800) 843-9948
TDD: (800) 892-8622
Fax: (701) 328-2040
E-mail: tbooks@nd.gov
Web site: http://library.nd.gov/disability
    services.html
Hours of Operation: 8:00–5:00 M–F
Serves: North Dakota; Braille readers receive
    service from Utah.

Ohio
Regional Library
Library for the Blind and Physically Handicapped
Cleveland Public Library
17121 Lake Shore Boulevard
Cleveland, OH 44110-4006
Librarian: Barbara T. Mates
Telephone: (216) 623-2911
Toll-free (In-state): (800) 362-1262
Fax: (216) 623-7036
E-mail: Barbara.Mates@cpl.org or
    LBPH@cpl.org
Web site: http://lbph.cpl.org/
Hours of Operation: 9:00–5:00 M–F
Serves: Allen, Ashland, Ashtabula, Auglaize,
    Belmont, Carroll, Champaign, Columbiana,
    Coshocton, Crawford, Cuyahoga, Darke,
    Defiance, Delaware, Erie, Franklin, Fulton,
    Geauga, Guernsey, Hancock, Hardin, Harrison,
    Henry, Holmes, Huron, Jefferson, Knox, Lake,
    Licking, Logan, Lorain, Lucas, Mahoning,
    Marion, Medina, Mercer, Morrow, Ottawa,
    Paulding, Portage, Putman, Richland,
    Sandusky, Seneca, Shelby, Stark, Summit,
    Trumbull, Tuscarawas, Union, Van Wert,
    Wayne, Williams, Wood, and Wyandot counties

Regional Library
The Public Library of Cincinnati and Hamilton
    County
Library for the Blind and Physically Handicapped
800 Vine Street
Cincinnati, OH 45202-2071

Librarian: Donna Foust
Telephone: (513) 369-6999
Toll-free (In-state): (800) 582-0335
TDD: (513) 369-3372
Fax: (513) 369-3111
E-mail: lb@cincinnatilibrary.org or
  donna.foust@cincinnatilibrary.org
Web site: http://www.cincinnatilibrary.org/
  main/lb.asp
Hours of Operation: 8:00–9:00 M–W;
  9:00–6:00 Th–Sat; 1:00–5:00 Sun
Serves: Adams, Athens, Brown, Butler, Clark,
  Clermont, Clinton, Fairfield, Fayette, Gallia,
  Greene, Hamilton, Highland, Hocking,
  Jackson, Lawrence, Madison, Meigs, Miami,
  Monroe, Montgomery, Morgan, Muskingum,
  Noble, Perry, Pickaway, Pike, Preble, Ross,
  Scioto, Vinton, Warren, and Washington counties

Oklahoma

Regional Library
Oklahoma Library for the Blind and Physically
  Handicapped
300 Northeast 18th Street
Oklahoma City, OK 73105
Librarian: Paul Adams
Telephone: (405) 521-3514 and (405) 522-0516
Toll-free (In-state): (800) 523-0288
TDD: (405) 521-4672
Fax: (405) 521-4582
E-mail: library@drs.state.ok.us
Web site: http://www.library.state.ok.us/
Hours of Operation: 8:00–5:00 M–F
Serves: Oklahoma; Braille readers receive
  service from Utah.

Oregon

Regional Library
Talking Book and Braille Services
Oregon State Library
250 Winter Street NE
Salem, OR 97301-3950
Librarian: Susan B. Westin
Telephone: (503) 378-3849 and (503) 378-5435
Toll-free (In-state): (800) 452-0292
TDD: (800) 735-2900
Fax: (503) 588-7119
E-mail: tbabs.info@state.or.us or
  susan.b.westin@state.or.us

Web site: http://TBABS.org
Hours of Operation: 8:00–5:00 M–F
Serves: Oregon; Braille readers receive
  service from Utah.

Pennsylvania

Regional Library
Library for the Blind and Physically Handicapped
Free Library of Philadelphia
P.O. Box 1194
Philadelphia, PA 19105
Librarian (acting): Nancy M. Laskowski
Telephone: (215) 683-3213
Toll-free (In-state): (800) 222-1754
Fax: (215) 683-3211
E-mail: flpblind@freelibrary.org
Web site: http://lbph.library.phila.gov/
Hours of Operation: 9:00–5:00 M–F
Serves: Bradford, Cumberland, Lycoming,
  Northumberland, Perry, Snyder, Sullivan, York,
  and all other counties in eastern Pennsylvania;
  Braille readers in Delaware, all of Pennsyl-
  vania, and West Virginia

Regional Library
Library for the Blind and Physically Handicapped
Carnegie Library of Pittsburgh
Leonard C. Staisey Building
4724 Baum Boulevard
Pittsburgh, PA 15213-1389
Librarian: Kathleen Kappel
Telephone: (412) 687-2440
Toll-free (In-state): (800) 242-0586
Fax: (412) 687-2442
E-mail: lbph@carnegielibrary.org
Web site: http://www.carnegielibrary.org/lbph
Hours of Operation: 9:00–5:00 M–F
Serves: Adams, Centre, Clinton, Franklin,
  Huntingdon, Juniata, Mifflin, Tioga, Warren,
  and all other counties in western Pennsylvania;
  Braille readers receive service from Philadelphia.

Puerto Rico

Regional Library
Puerto Rico Regional Library for the Blind
  and Physically Handicapped
520 Ponce de Leon Avenue, Suite 2
San Juan, PR 00901
Librarian: Igri Enriquez

Telephone: (787) 723-2519
Toll-free (In-state): (800) 981-8008
Fax: (787) 721-8177
E-mail: enriquezri@de.gobierno.pr
Web site: www.bibliotecaregionalparaciegos.com
Hours of Operation: 8:00–4:30 M–F
Serves: Puerto Rico

Rhode Island
Regional Library
Talking Books Plus
Office of Library and Information Services
One Capitol Hill
Providence, RI 02908
Librarian: Andrew Egan
Telephone: (401) 574-9310
TDD: (800) 745-6575
Fax: (401) 574-9320
E-mail: tbplus@olis.ri.gov
Web site: http://www.olis.ri.gov/tbp/
Hours of Operation: 8:00–4:00 M–F
Serves: Rhode Island; Braille readers
 receive service from Massachusetts.

South Carolina
Regional Library
South Carolina State Library
Talking Book Services
P.O. Box 821
Columbia, SC 29202-0821
Librarian: Pamela Davenport
Telephone: (803) 734-4611
Toll-free (In-state): (800) 922-7818
TDD: (803) 734-7298
Fax: (803) 734-4610
E-mail: tbsbooks@statelibrary.sc.gov or
 pdavenport@statelibrary.sc.gov
Web site: http://www.statelibrary.sc.gov
Hours of Operation: 8:30–5:00 M–F
Serves: South Carolina; Braille readers
 receive service from Utah

South Dakota
Regional Library
South Dakota Braille and Talking Book Library
State Library Building
800 Governors Drive
Pierre, SD 57501-2294
Librarian: Daniel W. Boyd

Telephone: (605) 773-3131
Toll-free (In-state): (800) 423-6665
Fax: (605) 773-6962
E-mail: dan.boyd@state.sd.us
Web site: http://www.sdstatelibrary.com/
 b&tb/index.htm
Hours of Operation: 8:00–5:00 M–F
Serves: South Dakota; Braille readers
 receive service from Utah.

Tennessee
Regional Library
Tennessee Library for the Blind and
 Physically Handicapped
Tennessee State Library and Archives
403 Seventh Avenue North
Nashville, TN 37243-0313
Librarian: Ruth Hemphill
Telephone: (615) 741-3915
Toll-free (In-state): (800) 342-3308
Fax: (615) 532-8856
E-mail: tlbph.tsla@state.tn.us or
 Ruth.Hemphill@state.tn.us
Web site: http://www.tennessee.gov/tsla/lbph/
Hours of Operation: 8:00–4:30 M–F
Serves: Tennessee

Texas
Regional Library
Texas State Library and Archives Commission
P.O. Box 12927
Austin, TX 78711-2927
Librarian: Ava M. Smith
Telephone: (512) 463-5458 and (512) 452-7306
Toll-free (In-state): (800) 252-9605
Fax: (512) 936-0685
E-mail: tbp.services@tsl.state.tx.us or
 amsmith@tsl.state.tx.us
Web site: http://www.texastalkingbooks.org
Hours of Operation: 8:00–5:00 M–F
Serves: Texas

U.S. Virgin Islands
Regional Library
Virgin Islands Library for the Visually and
 Physically Handicapped
3012 Golden Rock
Christiansted, VI 00820
Librarian: Letitia Gittens

Telephone: (340) 772-2250
Fax: (340) 772-3545
E-mail: reglib@vipowernet.net
Web site: http://www.library.gov.vi
Hours of Operation: 8:00–5:00 M–F
Serves: U.S. Virgin Islands

Utah
Regional Library
Utah State Library Division
Program for the Blind and Disabled
250 North 1950 West, Suite A
Salt Lake City, UT 84116-7901
Librarian: Bessie Y. Oakes
Telephone: (801) 715-6789
Toll-free (In-state): (800) 662-5540
TDD: (801) 715-6721
Fax: (801) 715-6767
E-mail: blind@utah.gov or boakes@utah.gov
Web site: http://blindlibrary.utah.gov/
Hours of Operation: 7:00–6:00 M–Th
Serves: Utah and Wyoming; Braille readers
   in Alabama, Alaska, Arizona, Georgia, Idaho,
   Illinois, Kansas, Louisiana, Mississippi,
   Montana, Nebraska, Nevada, New Mexico,
   North Dakota, Oklahoma, Oregon, South
   Carolina, South Dakota, and Wisconsin

Vermont
Regional Library
Vermont Department of Libraries
Special Services Unit
578 Paine Turnpike North
Berlin, VT 05602
Librarian: Teresa R. Faust
Telephone: (802) 828-3273
Toll-free (In-state): (800) 479-1711
Fax: (802) 828-2199
E-mail: ssu@mail.dol.state.vt.us
Web site: http://libraries.vermont.gov/libraries/ssu
Hours of Operation: 7:45–4:30 M–F
Serves: Vermont; Braille readers receive
   service from Massachusetts

Virginia
Regional Library
Virginia Library and Resource Center
Virginia Department for the Blind and
   Vision Impaired

395 Azalea Avenue
Richmond, VA 23227-3633
Librarian: Barbara N. McCarthy
Telephone: (804) 371-3661
Toll-free (In-state): (800) 552-7015
TDD: (804) 371-3661
Fax: (804) 371-3328
E-mail: barbara.mccarthy@dbvi.virginia.gov
Web site: http://www.vdbvi.org/lrcservices.htm
Hours of Operation: 8:15–5:00 M–F
Serves: Virginia

Subregional Library
Alexandria Library-Beatley Central
Talking Book Service
5005 Duke Street
Alexandria, VA 22304-2903
Librarian: Loni McCaffrey
Telephone: (703) 519-5911
TDD: (703) 519-5918
Fax: (703) 519-5916
E-mail: lmccaffrey@alexandria.lib.va.us
Web site: http://www.alexandria.lib.
   va.us/main/talking_book.html
Hours of Operation: 9:00–5:00 M–F
Serves: City of Alexandria

Subregional Library
Talking Book Service
Arlington County Subregional Library
1015 North Quincy Street
Arlington, VA 22201
Librarian: Lisbeth S. Goldberg
Telephone: (703) 228-6333
TDD: (703) 228-6320
Fax: (703) 228-7720
E-mail: talkingbooks@arlingtonva.us
Web site: http://www.arlingtonva.us/
   Departments/Libraries/outreach/Libraries
   OutreachSpecialNeeds.aspx
Hours of Operation: 9:00–5:00 M–F
Serves: Arlington County

Subregional Library
Access Services
Fairfax County Public Library
12000 Government Center Parkway
Suite 123
Fairfax, VA 22035-0012

Librarian: Janice Kuch
Telephone: (703) 324-8380
TDD: (703) 324-8365
Fax: (703) 324-8386
E-mail: access@fairfaxcounty.gov
Web site: http://www.fairfaxcounty.gov/
    library/branches/as/default.htm
Hours of Operation: 8:00–5:00 M–F
Serves: Fairfax County; cities of Fairfax
    and Falls Church

Subregional Library
Newport News Subregional Library for the
    Blind and Physically Handicapped
Newport News, VA 23601
Serves: James City and York counties; cities
    of Newport News and Williamsburg

Subregional Library
Roanoke Public Library
Talking Book Services
2607 Salem Turnpike NW
Roanoke, VA 24017-5397
Librarian: Gary Rushbrooke
Telephone: (540) 853-2648
Toll-free (In-state): (800) 528-2342
Fax: (540) 853-1030
E-mail: melrose.library@roanokeva.gov or
    gary.rushbrooke@roanokeva.gov
Web site: http://www.roanokegov.
    com/library/talking.html
Hours of Operation: 10:00–6:00 M, T, Th;
    10:00–8:00 W; 10:00–5:00 F–Sat
Serves: Alleghany, Botetourt, Craig, and Roanoke
    counties; cities of Clifton Forge, Covington,
    Roanoke, and Salem

Subregional Library
Bayside and Special Services Library, Department
    of Public Libraries
936 Independence Boulevard
Virginia Beach, VA 23455
Librarian: Carolyn Caywood
Telephone: (757) 385-2684 and (757) 385-2685
TDD: (757) 385-2690
Fax: (757) 464-6741
E-mail: LIBSSBH@vbgov.com or
    pjbrown@vbgov.com
Hours of Operation: 10:00–9:00 M–Th;
    10:00–5:00 F–Sat

Serves: Accomack, Isle of Wight, Northampton,
    and Southampton and Sussex counties; cities of
    Chesapeake, Norfolk, Portsmouth, Suffolk, and
    Virginia Beach

Subregional Library
Talking Book Center
Staunton Public Library
1 Churchville Avenue
Staunton, VA 24401
Librarian: Oakley Pearson
Telephone: (540) 885-6215
Toll-free (In-state): (800) 995-6215
Fax: (540) 332-3906
E-mail: pearsonjo@ci.staunton.va.us or
    talkingbooks@ci.staunton.va.us
Web site: http://www.talkingbookcenter.org
Hours of Operation: 9:00–5:00 M–F
Serves: Augusta, Bath, Highland, Rockbridge,
    and Rockingham counties; cities of Buena
    Vista, Harrisonburg, Lexington, Staunton,
    and Waynesboro

Subregional Library
Fredericksburg Area Subregional Library
Central Rappahannock Regional Library
1201 Caroline Street
Fredericksburg, VA 22401
Librarian: Nancy Buck
Telephone: (540) 372–1144
Toll-free (In-state): (800) 628–4807
TDD: (540) 371–9165
Fax: (540) 373–9411
E-mail: nbuck@crrl.org or esolka@crrl.org
Web site: http://www.librarypoint.org/
Hours of Operation: 9:00–5:30 M–F
Serves: Fredericksburg, Prince William,
    Spotsylvania, Stafford, and Westmoreland
    counties

Washington
Regional Library
Washington Talking Book and Braille Library
2021 Ninth Avenue
Seattle, WA 98121-2783
Librarian: Danielle King
Telephone: (206) 615-0400
Toll-free (In-state): (800) 542-0866
TDD: (206) 615-0418
Fax: (206) 615-0437

E-mail: wtbbl@secstate.wa.gov
Web site: http://www.wtbbl.org
Hours of Operation: 8:30–5:00 M–F
Serves: Washington

West Virginia
Regional Library
West Virginia Library
Commission—Special Libraries
Blind and Physically Handicapped Services
Cultural Center
1900 Kanawha Boulevard East
Charleston, WV 25305-0620
Librarian: Donna B. Calvert
Telephone: (304) 558-4061
Toll-free (In-state): (800) 642-8674
Fax: (304) 558-6016
E-mail: talkbks@wvlc.lib.wv.us or
    mathenyt@wvlc.lib.wv.us
Web site: http://librarycommission.
    lib.wv.us/vimpaired.html
Hours of Operation: 8:30–5:00 M–F
Serves: West Virginia; Braille readers receive
    service from Philadelphia, Pennsylvania.

Subregional Library
Services for the Blind and Physically Handicapped
Cabell County Public Library
455 Ninth Street Plaza
Huntington, WV 25701
Librarian: Vicky Woods
Telephone: (304) 528-5700
TDD: (304) 528-5694
Fax: (304) 528-5866
E-mail: tbooks@cabell.lib.wv.us
Web site: http://cabell.lib.wv.us/
    pages/talkbook.htm
Hours of Operation: 9:00–5:00 M–F
Serves: Cabell, Mason, Mingo, Putnam, and
    Wayne counties

Subregional Library
Services for the Blind and Physically Handicapped

Parkersburg and Wood County Public Library
3100 Emerson Avenue
Parkersburg, WV 26104-2414
Librarian: Michael Hickman
Telephone: (304) 420-4587
Fax: (304) 420-4589
E-mail: hickmanm@.park.lib.wv.us
Web site: http://parkersburg.lib.wv.us
Hours of Operation: 9:00–5:00 M–F
Serves: Calhoun, Jackson, Pleasants, Ritchie,
    Roane, Tyler, Wirt, and Wood counties

Subregional Library
West Virginia School for the Blind Library
301 East Main Street
Romney, WV 26757
Librarian: Mona Childs
Telephone: (304) 822-4894
Fax: (304) 822-4896
E-mail: mchilds@access.k12.wv.us
Hours of Operation: 8:00–5:00 M, W, F;
    8:00–8:00 T, Th
Serves: Berkeley, Grant, Hampshire, Hardy,
    Jefferson, Mineral, Morgan, and Pendleton
    counties

Wisconsin
Regional Library
Wisconsin Regional Library for the Blind
    and Physically Handicapped
813 West Wells Street
Milwaukee, WI 53233-1436
Librarian: Meredith Wittmann
Telephone: (414) 286-3045
Toll-free (In-state): (800) 242-8822
TDD: (414) 286-3548
Fax: (414) 286-3102
E-mail: mawittm@milwaukee.gov or
    lbph@milwaukee.gov
Web site: http://dpi.wi.gov/rll/wrlbph/
Hours of Operation: 9:00–5:00 M–F
Serves: Wisconsin; Braille readers receive
    service from Utah.

APPENDIX B

Three Library Policies
for Rules of Conduct

BERKELEY PUBLIC LIBRARY

(Adopted by the Board of Library Trustees 4/88 Revised 8/91, 9/95, 1/97, 9/02, 12/06, 12/07, 12/9)

These rules of conduct are for the comfort, safety and protection of all library patrons and library staff. Library staff and library security guards will firmly and courteously enforce these rules. We ask your cooperation in maintaining an environment conducive to enjoyable use of the Library for all. Dangerous, destructive or criminal conduct, including but not limited to the following, will not be tolerated:

- Physical abuse or assault;
- Fighting or challenging to fight;
- Making violent and threatening statements;
- Engaging in or soliciting any sexual act; and
- Damaging or destroying library property.

145

Any patron displaying any of these behaviors will be instructed to leave the Library immediately. Police will be called and appropriate legal action will follow. In addition, based on the severity of the situation, a suspension of library privileges for up to one year will be applied without advanced warning or prior suspension.

The following behaviors are also prohibited:

- Using harassing or insulting language.
- Leaving children under the age of eight (8) unattended by a parent or authorized adult.
- Blocking library entrances, ramps or exits, with animals, bicycles, strollers, etc.
- Participating in any activity in the Library or at public entrances/exits which interferes with any person's safety or egress.
- Entering Library with animals other than service animals authorized by law.
- Entering Library with bicycles, or riding skates, scooters, skateboards, etc.
- Smoking, eating or drinking.
- Being under the influence of alcohol or drugs to the extent that one is unable to exercise care for one's own safety or the safety of others.
- Lying on the floor or sleeping.
- Unreasonable use of rest rooms, including laundering and bathing.
- Exuding offensive, pervasive odors, including pervasive fragrances caused by perfume or other scented products.
- Disturbing or annoying anyone with loud and/or unreasonable noise, including using electronic equipment at a volume that disturbs others.
- Petitioning, soliciting or selling merchandise or services without written permission from the Director of Library Services.
- Personally monopolizing Library space, seating, tables or equipment to the exclusion of other patrons or staff.
- Fraudulent use of another's Library card and/or number for any purpose, including to reserve or use computers.
- Refusing to leave the Library and/or otherwise follow staff or law enforcement directions during emergency evacuation.
- Failing to wear shirt/top, pants/skirt, or shoes.

Any patrons displaying these behaviors will be addressed in the following manner:

First violation: Initial warning, given copy of Library Rules of Conduct.
Second violation: library privileges suspended for one day.
Third violation: library privileges suspended for seven days.
Fourth violation: library privileges suspended for up to one year.

If you observe anyone violating any of these rules of conduct, please inform either a security guard or a library staff member.

PLAINFIELD-GUILFORD TOWNSHIP PUBLIC LIBRARY

Patron Behavior Policy

(Adopted June 2002 by the Board of Trustees of the Plainfield-Guilford Township Public Library; revised November 2008)

Welcome to the Plainfield-Guilford Township Public Library. We ask your cooperation in maintaining an environment conducive to reading, studying and information gathering, as well as providing for the enjoyable use of the library for every patron. These rules are posted to protect the health, safety, welfare and rights of all patrons. Patron, however, are responsible for their behavior personal items and personal effects.

While on library property, the following behaviors and or actions are unacceptable:

- Bringing weapons onto library property.
- Damaging, misusing, monopolizing or vandalizing library facilities, equipment or materials.
- Removing library materials without properly checking them out.
- Abandoning, leaving or neglecting children or otherwise violating the Safe Child Policy.
- Harassing other library users or library staff including, but not limited to, excessive conversation, unwelcome advances or verbal, physical or sexual abuse.
- Possessing or being under the influence of alcohol or illegal controlled substances.
- Using tobacco products, having food or drink in restricted areas, or indulging in habitual sleeping.
- Using radios, televisions or CD/Tape players audible to others.
- Using cell phones in the main library. (Cell phones may be used in the lobby or upper mezzanine and hallway.)
- Selling, soliciting or panhandling (approaching patrons or staff members with items for sale or pleas for donations.)
- Distributing or posting printed materials or literature without prior director approval.
- Bringing bicycles into the library or using skateboards in the library.
- Blocking any entrance, aisle or exit.
- Bringing in animals except service dogs without prior director approval.
- Bringing in bulky items, including but not limited to sleeping bags, suitcases or large duffle bags.
- Using restrooms improperly, including but not limited to bathing or shaving.
- Being in the library before or after business hours without the written permission of the library director or his/her designee.

- Being a nuisance to others with offensive bodily hygiene.
- Entering office/workroom areas unless invited by a staff member or with prior written permission of the director.
- Indulging in a disturbance of the peace by loud or aggressive behavior, running, profanity, indecent or obscene language, or abusive language.
- Engaging in any indecent or obscene conduct or making any indecent exposure of one's person.
- Engaging in acts which are subject to prosecution under criminal codes of law.

If a library user chooses not to follow the library's Patron Behavior Policy, the user will be asked to correct the unacceptable behavior. If the behavior continues, the user will be asked to leave the library. Law enforcement will be called if the user refuses to leave.

PROHIBITIONS BY LIBRARY POLICY, ST. LOUIS PUBLIC LIBRARY

. . . in addition, it is the policy of the St. Louis Public Library:

To prohibit the access/presence by non staff to any non public areas, unless accompanied by a staff member.

To prohibit the consumption of food and beverages in the SLPL, except as authorized by the Library for specified occasions, or in specified areas of the Library.

To ban animals from the Library except for assist animals and as authorized for special events by SLPL Administration.

To prohibit all campaigning, petitioning, interviewing, survey taking, photography or video taping, soliciting or sales in library buildings and on library property without written permission from library administration.

To require that patrons wear shirts and shoes at all times in the Library.

To ban conversation and other sounds in louder volume than the general noise level of the area of the building at that time. Loud or boisterous behavior, running and foul or abusive language will not be tolerated.

This policy does not prohibit quiet conversation between patrons or staff or conversation and sounds required to carry on SLPL programs or business.

To require that sound equipment be operated at a volume which does not disturb other library users.

To prohibit sleeping, bathing, laundry or other inappropriate behavior in SLPL facilities.

To prohibit patrons from putting their feet on library furniture.

To prohibit littering on all SLPL properties.

To prohibit begging or soliciting.

Persons who violate the statutes, ordinances and rules listed above are subject to the withholding of SLPL privileges as follows:

First Offense: Patron will be evicted from SLPL and prohibited from returning for the remainder of the day.

Second Offense: Patron will be evicted from SLPL and SLPL privileges will be revoked for a period of one week.

Repeat Offenses: SLPL privileges will be revoked for a period of six months.

REFERENCES

Ageless Project, The. Available at http://jenett.org.ageless

Alliance for Technology Access. 2002. "Starting Points: Eliminating Barriers to People with Disabilities." Available at: http://www.ataccess.org/resources/acaw/documents/Starting_Points_v2.1_accessible.pdf

Alliance for Technology Access. n.d. "About the ATA." Available at: http://www.ataccess.org/about/default.html

American Library Association. 2001. "Library Services for People with Disabilities Policy." Available at: http://www.ala.org/ala/mgrps/divs/ascla/asclaissues/libraryservices.cfm

Amesbury Public Library. 2008. "Requests for Accommodations for Library Programs." Available at: http://www.amesburylibrary.org/Accommodations.pdf

Association of Assistive Technology Act Programs. n.d. Available at: http://www.ataporg.org/atap/projects.php?id=aboutus

Australian Library and Information Association. 2000. "Guidelines for Australian Home Library Services." Available at: http://www.alia.org.au/policies/home.library.service.html

Bartiméus Accessibility Foundation. 2006. "Gaming with a Physical Disability." Available at: http://www.accessibility.nl/games/index.php?pagefile=motoric

Bean, Carol. n.d. "Computers, Older Adults, and Libraries." Available at: http://beanworks.clbean.com/computers-older-adults-and-libraries/

Bean, Carol, and Laven, Michael. 2003. "Adapting to Seniors: Computer Training for Older Adults." Available at: http://dlist.sir.arizona.edu/260/01/Adapting_to_Seniorsv2.doc

Berkeley Public Library. 1988. "Rules of Conduct." Available at: http://www.berkeleypubliclibrary.org/about_the_library/policies.php

Berry, John N. III. 2008. "Best Small Library in America 2008: Chelsea District Library—A Michigan Model." *Library Journal, 2.* Available at: http://www.libraryjournal.com/article/CA6523445.html

Bi-Folkal Productions. n.d. "The Ideas Behind Bi-Folkal Kits." Available at: http://www.bifolkal.org/bf_kitintro.html

Bruyere, Susanne M., and Houtenville, Andrew J. 2006. "Use of Statistics from National Data Sources to Inform Rehabilitation Program Planning, Evaluation, and Advocacy." *Rehabilitation Counseling Bulletin, 50* (Fall): pp. 46–58.

Burgstahler, Sheryl. 2002. "Universal Access: Making Library Resources Accessible to Persons with Disabilities." Available at: http://www.washington.edu/doit/UA/PRESENT/libres.html

Cahalan, Brigid. 2008. "Wisdom and Wii at the Public Library." Available at: http://drupal02.nypl.org/blogs/2008/12/15/wisdom-and-wii-public-library

California State Library. 2007. "Transforming Life After 50: Public Libraries and Baby Boomers." Available at: http://transforminglifeafter50.org/files/TLAFOverviewAgendaGoals.pdf

Carrier, Kathy. 2008. "Games Offer Brain Workouts." *Grand Rapids Press.* Available at: http://blog.mlive.com/grpress/2008/02/games_offer_brain_workouts.html

Caulton, Jane. 2006. *NLS at 75: National Program for Blind Readers Examines Its Past and Looks toward Its Future* (Information Bulletin 65, no. 11 260-2 N 2006). Washington, DC: Library of Congress.

Chelsea District Library. 2008. "Homebound Services." Available at: http://www.chelsea.lib.mi.us/homebound.htm

Cohen, Gene. 2006. *The Mature Mind: The Positive Power of the Aging Brain*. New York: Basic Books.

Dahms-Stinson, Nancee, ed. 2002. *Serving Seniors: A Resource Manual for Missouri Libraries*. Jefferson City, MO: Missouri State Library.

Deines-Jones, Courtney. 1996. "Access to Library Internet Services for Patrons with Disabilities: Pragmatic Considerations for Developers." Available at: http://people.rit.edu/easi/itd/itdv02n4/article5.htm

DeLatte, Monique, ed. 2008. "Library Accessibility—What You Need to Know." Available at: http://www.ala.org/ala/mgrps/divs/ascla/asclaprotools/accessibilitytipsheets/default.cfm

Franklin Institute. 2004. "Improve Your Brain." Available at: http://www.fi.edu/learn/brain/exercise.html

Gemmer, Theresa. 2003. "Homebound Services: Old Ways and New Ways." *Bookmobile and Outreach Services* 6(2), 35–39.

Gritten, Tim. 2008. "Seniors and Students All Love Playing the Library's Wii Games." *Marketing Library Services* 22(3). Available at: http://www.infotoday.com/mls/may08/Gritten.shtml

Gwinn, Eric. 2007. "Disabled Gamers Want More Than 'Fluffy' Choices." *Chicago Tribune*. Available at: http://www.aionline.edu/about-us/news/ChicagoTribFlorio.pdf

Harmer, Bill. "Library Services to Seniors." Presentation, Missouri State Library Summer Institute, Columbia, MO, 2008.

Health Care for the Homeless Clinicians' Network. 2000. "Mental Illness, Chronic Homelessness: An American Disgrace." Available at: http://www.nhchc.org/Network/HealingHands/2000/October2000HealingHands.pdf

Hennepin County Library. 2008. "Art Abilities Gallery Open on Oct. 5, Showcases Artwork by Artists with Disabilities." Available at: http://www.hclib.org/pub/info/newsroom/index.cfm?ID=123&Type=News

Hennepin County Library. n.d.a "Accessibility." Available at: http://hclib.org/pub/info/accessibility.cfm

Hennepin County Library. n.d.b "Hennepin County Library Makes House Calls!" Available at: http://www.hclib.org/pub/info/Outreach/AHRapplication.cfm

Holmes County District Public Library. 2007. "Special Needs Lending Library." Available at: http://www.holmeslibrary.org/hctc

Jackson, Richard. 2007. "Building Health in Our Communities." Presentation at the Transforming Life After 50 Training Institute, Pasadena, CA. Available at: http://transforminglifeafter50.org/node/206

Julia L. Butterfield Memorial Library. n.d. "Americans with Disabilities Act Compliance Policy." Available at: http://midhudson.org/department/member_information/policy/ADA_coldspring.pdf

Kleiman, Allan. 2008. "Libraries, Older Adults, and Web 2.0." Presentation at Missouri state libraries, Springfield, Warrensburg, Moberly, and Jackson, MO. Available at: http://www.slideshare.net/allanmkleiman

LibriVox. n.d. "LibriVox Acoustical Liberation of Books in the Public Domain." Available at: http://librivox.org/

Mast, Dave. 2007. "Three Area Libraries Praised for Programs Created through Federal Grant Program." *The Holmes Bargain Hunter*.

Meredith College. 2009. "Disability Services Student Handbook: 2008–2009." Available at: http://www.meredith.edu/students/counsel/disability/documents/DS_Student_Handbook_08_09_000.pdf

Missouri Department of Mental Health. 2007. "Welcome." Available at: http://www.librarian411.org/

Missouri Department of Mental Health. 2009. "Library Services and Technology Act Grant." Available at: http://www.dmh.missouri.gov/mrdd/libservices/library.htm

Morales, Tom, Russ Holland, Mary Lester, and June Kailes. 2001. "Access Aware: Extending Your Reach to Persons with Disabilities." Available at: http://www.ataccess.org/resources/acaw/s00/s00.html

Morrissey, Patricia A., and Silverstein, Robert. 1989. "The Technology-Related Assistance for Individuals with Disabilities Act of 1988." Available at: http://findarticles.com/p/articles/mi_m0842/is_n2_v15/ai_8200899?tag=content;col1

Mortensen, Helle Arendrup, and Nielsen, Gyda Skat. 2007. *A Challenge for Public Libraries: Guidelines for Library Services to Persons with Dementia*. The Hague, Netherlands: IFLA Professional Reports.

Motsinger, Carol. 2007. "Libraries Offer More Services to Homeless." *USA Today*. Available at: http://www.usatoday.com/news/nation/2007–06–13-libraries_N.htm?csp=34

Murphy, Julie. 1999. "When the Rights of the Many Outweigh the Rights of the Few: The 'Legitimate' Versus the Homeless Patron in the Public Library." Available at: http://www.crowbold.com/homepage/homeless.htm

Nakao, Annie. 2005. "Oakland: Library Icons Help Those with Learning Disabilities Navigate the Shelves." *San Francisco Chronicle*. Available at: http://www.sfgate.com/cgi-bin/article.cgi?f=/c/a/2005/09/23/EBG82EO4KP1.DTL

National Association of State Units on Aging. 2008. "The Economic Crisis and Its Impact on State Aging Programs." Available at: http://www.nasua.org/documents/EconomicSurveyReport.pdf

National Center for Learning Disabilities. 2009. "Dyscalculia." Available at: http://www.ncld.org/ld-basics/ld-aamp-language/ld-aamp-math/dyscalculia

National Coalition for the Homeless. 2005. "Mental Illness and Homelessness." Available at: http://www.nhchc.org/ShelterHealth/ToolKitD/D2MentalIllnessand92836.pdf

National Council on Disability. 2001. "National Disability Policy: A Progress Report, November 1999–November 2000." Available at: http://www.ncd.gov/newsroom/publications/2001/pdf/progressreport2000.pdf

National Institute of Mental Health. 2008. "The Numbers Count: Mental Disorders in America." Available at: http://www.nimh.nih.gov/health/publications/the-numbers-count-mental-disorders-in-america/index.shtml

National Institute of Mental Health. 2009. "The National Institute of Mental Health Strategic Plan." Available at: http://www.mentalhealth.gov/about/strategic-planning-reports/index.shtml

National Institute of Mental Health. n.d. "Mental Health Topics." Available at: http://www.nimh.nih.gov/health/topics/index.shtml

National Institute of Neurological Disorders and Stroke. n.d.a "NINDS Learning Disabilities Information Page." Available at: http://www.ninds.nih.gov/disorders/learningdisabilities/learningdisabilities.htm

National Institute of Neurological Disorders and Stroke. n.d.b "Tourette Syndrome Fact Sheet." Available at: http://www.ninds.nih.gov/disorders/tourette/detail_tourette.htm

National Institute on Aging and the National Libraries of Medicine. 2001. "Making Your Web Site Senior Friendly." Available at: http://www.nih.gov/icd/od/ocpl/resources/wag/documents/checklist.pdf

National Library Services for the Blind and Physically Handicapped. 2004. "NLS launches 10^2 Talking Book Club." *News, 35*(4). Available at: http://www.loc.gov/nls/newsletters/news/2004/oct_dec.html

National Library Services for the Blind and Physically Handicapped. 2005. "Missouri Inducts Ten New Members into 10^2 Club on National Centenarian Day." Available at: http://rs7.loc.gov/nls/10squared/missouri.html

National Library Services for the Blind and Physically Handicapped. 2006. "Eligibility for Service." Available at: http://www.loc.gov/nls/eligible.html

National Library Services for the Blind and Physically Handicapped. 2007. "Downloading Digital Talking Books from NLS." Available at: http://www.nfbnet.org/pipermail/dtb-talk_nfbnet.org/2007-September/002047.html

National Library Services for the Blind and Physically Handicapped. n.d. "That All May Read." Available at: http://www.loc.gov/nls/

National Network of Libraries of Medicine. 2006. "About the National Network of Libraries of Medicine (NN/LM)." Available at: http://nnlm.gov/about/

National Network of Libraries of Medicine. 2008. "Health Literacy." Available at: http://nnlm.gov/outreach/consumer/hlthlit.html

New Jersey State Library. 1999. "Equal Access to Information: Libraries Serving People With Disabilities." Available at: http://www.njstatelib.org/LDB/Disabilities/dsequa2.php

Office of Juvenile Justice and Delinquency Prevention. 1998. "Summary: Guidelines for the Screening of Persons Working with Children, the Elderly, and Individuals with Disabilities in Need of Support." Available at: http://ojjdp.ncjrs.org/pubs/guidelines/contents.html

"Parade of Freaks." 2008. Available at: http://librarianwoes.wordpress.com/2008/01/02/parade-of-freaks

Pew Research Center. 2008. "Generations Online in 2009." Available at: http://www.pewinternet.org/Reports/2009/Generations-Online-in-2009.aspx

Plainfield-Guilford Township Public Library. 2002. "Patron Behavior Policy." Available at: http://www.plainfieldlibrary.net/librarybasics/librarypolicies.html

Powell, Ernie. 2007. "Boomers Health Care and Economic Security: It Isn't One Size Fits All." Presentation at the Transforming Life After 50 Training Institute, Pasadena, CA. Available at: http://transforminglifeafter50.org/node/325

Randolph County Public Library. 1998. "Randolph County Public Library Disruptive Behavior Policy." Available at: http://www.randolphlibrary.org/librarypolicies.htm

Reference and User Services Association of the American Library Association. 2008. "Guidelines for Library and Information Services to Older Adults." Available at: http://www.ala.org/ala/mgrps/divs/rusa/resources/guidelines/libraryservices. cfm

Satterfield, Brian. 2007. "How to Test a Web Site for Accessibility: A Step-by-Step Guide for Determining Whether Your Web Site Is Accessible to Persons with Disabilities." Available at: http://www.techsoup.org/binaries/files/How-to-Test-a-Web-Site-for-Accessibility.pdf

Schull, Diantha. 2007. "Lifelong Access: A Vision for Public Libraries." Presentation at the Transforming Life After 50 Training Institute, Pasadena, CA. Available at: http://transforminglifeafter50.org/node/201

Sheppard-Jones, Kathy. 2000. "Those of Us Dislabeled: A Guide to Awareness and Understanding." Available at: http://www.ihdi.uky.edu/pubs/General%20 Resources/Dislabled/dislabeled24.htm

Smith, Richard. 2009. "New 'Reader' Technology for Wolfner Patrons." Available at: http://www.sos.mo.gov/library/showme_libraries/0809_fall_winter.asp

Snow, Kathie. 2005. *Disability Is Natural: Revolutionary Common Sense for Raising Successful Children with Disabilities* (2nd ed.). Woodland Park, CO: BraveHeart Press.

Snow, Kathie. 2007. *101 Reproducible Articles for a New Disability Paradigm.* Woodland Park, CO: BraveHeart Press.

Snow, Kathie. 2008. "Question Yourself." Available at: http://www.disabilityisnatu ral.com/images/PDF/question.pdf

Snow, Kathie. 2009. "People First Language." Available at: http://www.disabilityis natural.com/images/PDF/pfl09.pdf

Snow, Kathie. n.d. "About Kathie Snow." Available at: http://www.disabilityisnatu ral.com/about/about-kathie-snow

St. Louis Public Library. 2000. "Appropriate Use of the Library." Available at: http:// www.slpl.org/slpl/library/Article240096442.asp

Substance Abuse and Mental Health Services Administration. 2003. "Homelessness—Provision of Mental Health and Substance Abuse Services." Available at: http:// mentalhealth.samhsa.gov/publications/allpubs/homelessness/

Tanner, Lindsey. 2008. "Break a Leg? Try 'Wiihabilitation': System Is Used for Patients Recovering from Strokes, Surgery." Available at: http://www.msnbc. msn.com/id/23070190/

Traverse Area District Library. n.d. "The Senior Corner." Available at: http://seniors. tcnet.org/

Twain, Mark. (1888). "Letter to George Bainton." Available at http://www.twain quotes.com/Word.html

Thornhill, Matt. 2007. "How Libraries Can Respond." Presentation at the Transforming Life After 50 Training Institute, Pasadena, CA. Available at: http:// transforminglifeafter50.org/node/208

University of Washington. n.d. "DO-IT." Available at: http://www.washington.edu/doit/

U.S. Census Bureau. 2000. "United States Census 2000." Available at: http://www. census.gov/dmd/www/pdf/d02p.pdf

U.S. Census Bureau. 2003. "Disability Status: 2000." Available at: http://www.census. gov/prod/2003pubs/c2kbr-17.pdf

U.S. Census Bureau. 2006. "Oldest Baby Boomers Turn 60!" Available at: http:// www.census.gov/Press-Release/www/releases/archives/facts_for_features_ special_editions/006105.html

U.S. Conference of Mayors. 2008. "Hunger and Homelessness Survey." Available at: http://usmayors.org/pressreleases/documents/hungerhomelessnessreport_121208.pdf

U.S. Department of Health and Human Services. 2005. "Children's Mental Health Facts: Attention Deficit/Hyperactivity Disorder." Available at: http://mentalhealth.samhsa.gov/publications/allpubs/SMA05-4059/

U.S. Department of Health and Human Services. 2007. "Quick Guide to Health Literacy and Older Adults." Available at: http://www.health.gov/communication/literacy/olderadults/literacy.htm

U.S. Department of Justice. 1996. "Commonly Asked Questions about Service Animals in Places of Business." Available at: http://www.ada.gov/qasrvc.htm

Walling, Linda Lucas. 2004. "Educating Students to Serve Information Seekers with Disabilities." *Journal of Education for Library and Information Science 45*(2), 137–48.

Wilton Library Association. n.d. "Senior Resources." Available at: http://www.wiltonlibrary.org/senior

Whitbeck, Faye. 2008. "Changing our Minds: Those with Mental Illness Need Understanding and Respect." The Daily Journal. Available at: http://www.ifallsdailyjournal.com/news/about-local-folks/changing-our-minds-those-mental-illness-need-understanding-and-respect-faye-w

INDEX

ABOUT THE AUTHORS

ANN ROBERTS has a MA in music from Louisiana State University and an MLS from the University of Pittsburgh. She is a certified archivist and currently serving as the adult services consultant in library development for the Missouri State Library. She is the author of *A Crash Course in Library Gift Programs: The Reluctant Curator's Guide to Caring for Archives, Books and Artifacts in a Library Setting* (Libraries Unlimited, 2007).

RICHARD J. SMITH has an MLS and PhD from the University of Pittsburgh and is the director of Wolfner Library for the Blind and Physically Handicapped for the state of Missouri. He is an early proponent of Internet usage, which resulted in the first online worldwide Internet training course called "Navigating the Internet," and a resulting best-selling book by the same title.